A Residence on the Shores of the Baltic. Described in a series of letters.

Elizabeth Rigby

A Residence on the Shores of the Baltic. Described in a series of letters. [By Elizabeth Rigby, afterwards Lady Eastlake.]
Rigby, Elizabeth
British Library, Historical Print Editions
British Library
1842
2 vol. ; 8°.
10106.df.15.

The BiblioLife Network

This project was made possible in part by the BiblioLife Network (BLN), a project aimed at addressing some of the huge challenges facing book preservationists around the world. The BLN includes libraries, library networks, archives, subject matter experts, online communities and library service providers. We believe every book ever published should be available as a high-quality print reproduction; printed on- demand anywhere in the world. This insures the ongoing accessibility of the content and helps generate sustainable revenue for the libraries and organizations that work to preserve these important materials.

The following book is in the "public domain" and represents an authentic reproduction of the text as printed by the original publisher. While we have attempted to accurately maintain the integrity of the original work, there are sometimes problems with the original book or micro-film from which the books were digitized. This can result in minor errors in reproduction. Possible imperfections include missing and blurred pages, poor pictures, markings and other reproduction issues beyond our control. Because this work is culturally important, we have made it available as part of our commitment to protecting, preserving, and promoting the world's literature.

GUIDE TO FOLD-OUTS, MAPS and OVERSIZED IMAGES

In an online database, page images do not need to conform to the size restrictions found in a printed book. When converting these images back into a printed bound book, the page sizes are standardized in ways that maintain the detail of the original. For large images, such as fold-out maps, the original page image is split into two or more pages.

Guidelines used to determine the split of oversize pages:

- Some images are split vertically; large images require vertical and horizontal splits.
- For horizontal splits, the content is split left to right.
- For vertical splits, the content is split from top to bottom.
- For both vertical and horizontal splits, the image is processed from top left to bottom right.

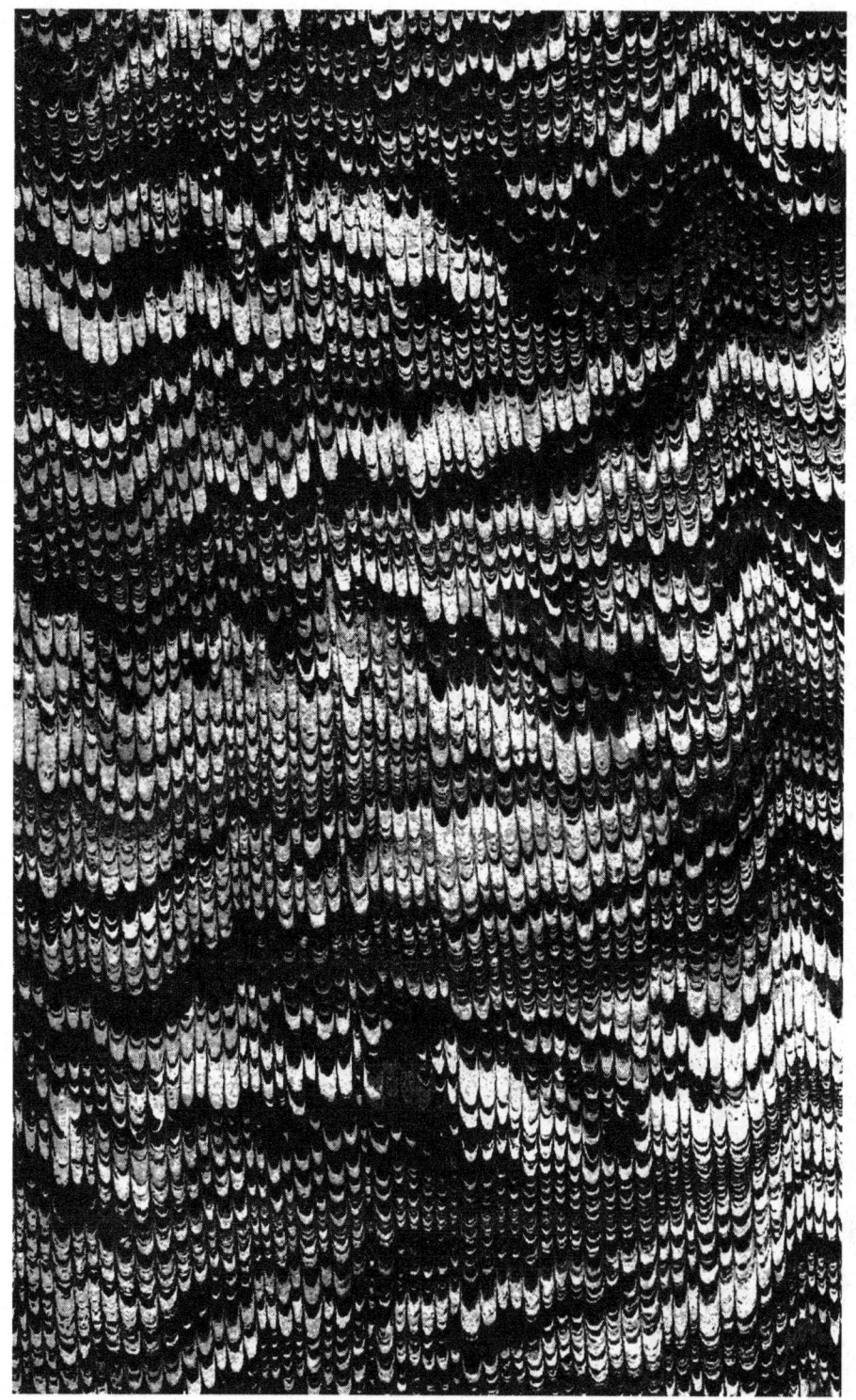

10100 оф 10

LETTERS

FROM THE

SHORES OF THE BALTIC.

SECOND EDITION.
WITH TWENTY ETCHINGS.

IN TWO VOLUMES.

VOL. II.

LONDON:
JOHN MURRAY, ALBEMARLE STREET.
1842.

LONDON:
Printed by WILLIAM CLOWES and SONS,
Stamford Street.

CONTENTS OF VOLUME II.

LETTER THE FOURTEENTH.

Depressing effects of the long winter—Hardships of the peasants—General state of health—Superstitions—The burthen of the poll-tax and recruitage system—Anecdotes of recruiting—Miseries of a Russian soldier's life—Advantages of the same—Sascha's trials of conscience—The Russian language—Literature of Russia—Foreigners' ideas of England—Languor of the season . . 1

LETTER THE FIFTEENTH.

Sudden burst of spring—Last sledging drive—Thaw in the town and thaw in the country—The Eisgang—Inundation—Rapidity of Nature's movements—Green fields and trees—Nightingales without sentiment—Family party—Introduction of a bride elect—Hermann B. 20

LETTER THE SIXTEENTH.

Early rising—Departure on a journey—Drive through a wild country—Diversities of taste in the situation of a residence—A Krug—Rosenthal—Boulder stones—Castle Lode, and the unfortunate Princess of Wirtemberg—A very hard bed—Leal—An accumulation of annoyances—The Wieck, and its seashore riches—Baron Ungern Sternberg—Count and Countess ——, and their seat at Linden—Anecdote of Peter the Great and his friend Menschikoff—The Castle of Habsal—Dagen girl—Odd collections—Riesenberg and the Baroness S. 37

LETTER THE SEVENTEENTH.

Bathing life at Reval—Custom-house troubles extraordinary—Voyage across the Gulf—Union of various nations—Approach to Helsingforst—A ball—Baroness K.—Shopping propensities of lady passengers—Granite beauties of Helsingforst—The Observatory—The Botanical Garden—An eventful dinner—Sweaborg—The Scheeren—Symptoms of smuggling—Return to Reval . 64

LETTER THE EIGHTEENTH.

Reval at Midsummer—Antiquities—Gates—Churches—Dance of Death—The Duke de Croy—Hôtel de Ville—Corps of the Schwarzen Häupter—Towers—Antiquities of the Domberg—Kotzebue—The Jahr Markt, and its varied population—Catherinthal—The water-party—Visit to a Russian man-of-war . 83

LETTER THE NINETEENTH.

Excessive heat—Gnats and gnat-bites—Sleepless nights—Ruins of Padis Kloster—Landrath R.—Baltisport—Leetz—The Island of Little Rogö—Unexpected encounter—Russian builders—A day in the woods—Family parties—Mode of salutation—Old-fashioned manners—Conversation—English pride and German pride—Jealousy of Russian tendencies—Marriages between Russians and Estonians 110

CONTENTS.

LETTER THE TWENTIETH.

Fall and its beauties—The daughters of Fall—The Countess mother—A gathering of all nations—Cuisine—Occupations—Varieties of scenes and languages—The château—Its various treasures—Russian church—In-door beauties and out-door beauties—Count C. and Princess V.—Salmon-fishing—Illuminations—Adventurous passage—Countess Rossi—Armen-Concert at Reval—Rehearsals—The Scena from the Freischütz—Return home . 142

LETTER THE TWENTY-FIRST.

Autumn Scenes—Separation from Estonia 174

LETTER THE TWENTY-SECOND.

Russia considered as a study—New Year's Eve—Peculiar family demonstrations—Bridge of Kisses—Routine of a Petersburg life—Oriental regiments, and Oriental physiognomy—Fête at the Winter Palace—Scene from the gallery of the Salle Blanche—Court costume—Display of diamonds—Masked ball at the theatre—The Emperor—The Héritier—The Grand Duke Michael—Masked ball at the Salle de Noblesse—Uses and abuses of masked balls in Russia 183

LETTER THE TWENTY-THIRD.

Chief houses of reception in St. Petersburg—Freedom of the Imperial Family—Restraint of the subject—Absence of etiquette—Ball at Prince Y.'s—Ball at Countess L.'s—Beauties of the high circles—Ball at Madame L.'s—General aspect of manners and morals—Dress—Servants—The Grand Duchess Helen . . 220

LETTER THE TWENTY-FOURTH.

Prince Pierre Volkonski—Count Benkendorff—Count Nesselrode—Taglioni—The Empress—Madame Allan—The Russian Theatre—The first Russian opera—Characteristics of the three classes of society in Russia—Power of the monarch—Railroad to Zarskoe Selo—The Great Palace—Reminiscences of the Emperor Alexander—The Emperor's Palace—The Arsenal—General impressions 245

LETTER THE TWENTY-FIFTH.

Visit to the Ateliers of Brülloff, Baron Klot, M. Jaques, M. Ladournaire—The Isaac's Church—M. le Maire—Gallery of Prince Belozelsky—Tauride Palace—Church of Smolna, and adjacent institutions—Procession of young girls in court carriages—Winter aspect of the streets—Night drives—Lent and farewell . 270

LETTERS FROM THE BALTIC

LETTER THE FOURTEENTH.

Depressing effects of the long Winter—Hardships of the peasants—General state of health—Superstitions—The burthen of the poll-tax and recruitage system—Anecdotes of recruiting—Miseries of a Russian soldier's life—Advantages of the same—Sascha's trials of conscience—The Russian language—Literature of Russia—Foreigners' ideas of England—Languor of the season.

April.

THIS is the season which tries the health and spirits of the native of a more genial clime. How long it is that our island has been clothed in green—how long it is that you have been enjoying sweet sights and scents in such profusion as almost to neglect these precious offerings, whilst we have sledged back to our country home over roads as hard with frost, and deeper with snow than ever, to find Nature as dry, frigid, and motionless as we left her ten weeks ago! It is said that the first rose presented to Sir Edward Parry, on returning from one of his voyages, he involuntarily seized and ate. From my own present voracious yearnings for some token of verdant life, however humble, I can quite comprehend such an act. How dependent is man! If the accustomed blessings be delayed but a few weeks, the soul pines, and even the physical powers languish as with the *mal du pays*. The sight of a violet would I believe affect me, as the sound of their native melodies did the home-sick Swiss. Our rooms, it is true, are decked with blooming exotics, but it is the green earth we long for.

The season, however, is unusually protracted, and the enervating effect of the spring air, which has long preceded its other attributes, is evident in the languor of the domestic animals around us. The little peasant horses, who turn off the Bahn up to their chests in the deep snow to make way for our better fed and less laden animals, can hardly drag themselves into the track again. The fodder is beginning to fail, and yet no sign appears of that change which is to remove these accumulated months of snow; for whatever of thaw the increasing height and power of the sun may effect in the day, the frost, Penelope-like, counteracts in the night; and the surface of the earth remains as deep hidden as ever beneath these swathings of cold cotton wool. The long days, the dazzling light, the unvaryingly beautiful weather, the prismatic hues on the western hemisphere on which the evening star shines like a pale spangle upon a robe of orient tints, all add but to longings they cannot assuage. Till Nature's renascence give life to these lovely elements, we embrace but a statue.

Now it is that the peasants claim our utmost help. If their sufferings be less sentimental than our own, they are also more positive. At the beginning of winter the peasant fares well, eats wholesome rye bread, and plenty of it. Towards spring, his stores, never well husbanded, begin to fail, and the coarse rye flour is eked out with a little chopped straw; but, when the season is thus prolonged, this position is reversed, and it is the straw which becomes the chief ingredient of the loaf which is to fill, not nourish, his body—so much so that on exposure to fire this wretched bread will ignite and blaze like a torch. This insufficient fare is often followed by an epidemic—typhus or scarlet fever. The latter especially is the scourge of the land, and almost invariably fatal to children; and villages are sometimes depopulated of their juvenile members, for those who struggle through the fever are carried off by subsequent dropsy. As for prompt medical attendance, how is that to be expected among a poor and widely-scattered population, which not even the highest classes in the land can command? Many a nobleman's family is situated a hundred wersts from medical aid, and thus four-and-twenty fatal hours will sometimes elapse which no skill can recover. Upon the whole, however, the average of health is very good. There are no such gaps among families,—no fading of such opening flowers as English parents follow to the grave,—no such heart-breaking bereavements of young mothers, who, when most dear and most needed, delegate their breath to the infant who has just received it; or rather, few are such instances among the whole colony of the noblesse, all known to each other, in comparison with the loss which in both these respects the narrow compass of my own connexion affords. In the department of pharmacy the medical men appear highly skilful and enlightened, though in that of chirurgery not equally advanced. The daring, successful skill of the famous operator Pyragoff of Dorpat, however, has been frequently evinced here, as his sphere of philanthropic practice may be said to include these three provinces. In accidents and simpler maladies, a village Esculapius is often resorted to, who will set a limb and open a vein as successfully as a regular practitioner; and as both patient and prescriber are equally under the influence of superstition, this enters largely both into means and cure.

The other day, a lady in the neighbourhood, whose adherence to ancient usages includes her among a class now fast fading from society, being attacked with erysipelas in the foot, sent for the wise man of the village to charm it away. A kind of Estonian Fakeer was announced, whom, in the first place, it required faith of no common kind to approach at all, and who, after various incantations, striking a light, &c., over the limb, broke silence by asking for a piece of bread and butter. "Cut him a thick slice, I dare say he is hungry," said the good soul, fumbling for her keys, and anxious to propitiate the oracle; and away ran the Mamiselle to the Schafferei, and returned with a thick octavo-volume slice, which under ordinary circumstances would have chased away all hunger to look at. This the old man took, but instead of applying his teeth to the task, commenced tracing the sign of the cross and other forms with his long nails through the thick butter; and when the surface was well marbled and furrowed with lines of dirt, solemnly made it over to his patient to eat,—and this, though somewhat taken by surprise, it is only just to add, she conscientiously did, but how the erysipelas fared in consequence I know not.

From the frequent succession of masters, I have alluded to before, it is as difficult to judge fairly of the Estonian peasant as of the child who is always changing school—a state of things which is not unseldom aggravated by the circumstance of a wealthy or indifferent Seigneur leaving his peasantry entirely at the mercy of a so-called *Disponent*, or bailiff; an individual who occupies much the same situation without, as a Mamselle within the house, and, like an Irish agent, too often grinds the one party and defrauds the other. The lower class of Germans here are a most disrespectable set, and not nearly so trusty, as the native Estonians whom they affect to despise. Some instances occur of Estonians who have raised themselves from the peasant's hut to a state of competence, retaining no indication of their origin save in their peculiar Estonian German; but, generally speaking, at best they are but a fretted nation, borne down by the double misery of poll-tax and liability to recruitage,—the one the price they pay for their breath, the other for their manhood. Happy the family where only girls are born, who offer the double advantage of working as hard, and paying less than the other sex. The present rate of *Kopf Steuer*, or poll-tax, is four roubles sixty copecks, or about four shillings English per head, not only upon the able-bodied man, but upon every chick and child of male kind—an enormous tax when the relative value of money is considered. A revision of the population takes place every sixteen years, and, if the household pay not for those born unto them in the interim, they do for those taken from them; therefore the crown is no loser, and the ill wind blows no good to the peasant.

The recruiting system falls especially hard upon those provinces tributary to Russia, but otherwise not Russianized. No matter how foreign and incongruous, all atoms that enter that vast crucible, the Russian army, are fused down to the same form. The Estonian, therefore, fares so much worse than the native Russian, in that he leaves not only kindred and home, but language, country, and religion, and furthermore an inherent taste for a pastoral life, which the Russian does not share. From the moment that the peasant of the Baltic provinces draws the fatal lot No. 1, he knows that he is a Russian, and, worse than that, a Russian soldier, and not only himself, but every son from that hour born to him; for, like the executioner's office in Germany, a soldier's life in Russia is hereditary. He receives no bounty money, on the contrary his parish is charged with the expense of his outfit to the amount of between thirty and forty roubles—his hair, which an Estonian regards as sacred, is cut to within a straw's breadth of his head; and amidst scenes of distress which have touched the sternest hearts, the Estonian shepherd leaves the home of his youth. If wars and climate and sickness and hardship spare him, he returns after four-and-twenty years of service— his language scarce remembered, his religion changed, and with not a rouble in his pocket— to seek his daily bread by his own exertions for the remainder of his life, or to be chargeable to his parish, who by this time have forgotten that he ever existed, and certainly wish he had never returned. Perhaps an order or two decorates him, or reaches him after his dismissal; but the worn-out Russian soldier has little pride in the tokens of that bravery which has consumed his health, strength, and best years, and earned him no maintenance when these are gone.

The age of liability is from twenty to thirty-five—the number at this time annually drawn five in a thousand. Each estate of five *Haken*— a measurement relating to amount of corn sown, and not to actual extent—can screen four *Recrutenfähige,* or liable subjects; no estate can screen more than twelve. This power of protection is engrossed principally by the house and stable servants—for your own valet, or coachman, unless you purchase his exemption, is just as liable as the rest. The price of exemption is a thousand roubles, or a hundred roubles a-year for fifteen years. If one year be omitted or delayed, the previous payments are annulled. Nor will the crown accept a man the less, and another suffers for his neighbour's better means. Besides purchase money, the only grounds for exemption consist in a personal defect, or a family of three children.

The father of two children is taken. At the last annual recruiting a peasant, already the father of one child and about to become that of another, drew the fatal lot, and with streaming eyes and trembling limbs was quitting the room to take leave of all dear to him, when the door burst open and his father, flinging himself on his neck, proclaimed him free. His wife had been confined of twins. With regard to the other cause for exemption, examples of voluntary maiming are not rare. A stonemason whom we observed chiselling a delicate piece of sculpture under the utmost strain of sight, for one eye was blinded with a cataract we strenuously urged to apply for medical aid, but smiling he replied, "I would not have two eyes for the world—now I can't be taken for a recruit."

On those estates where the population from some cause is not able to make up the necessary number of recruits, a child is delivered over and consigned to the military school at Reval. The crown must have its "pound of flesh." This substitute, however, it accepts most unwillingly, as each of these little *Cantonisten*, as they are termed, costs government at the rate of thirty copecks a-day, and not above one-third are reared for actual service. Such is the anxiety of the crown to enforce every means of securing men for the army, that the moment a soldier's wife gives birth to a son the parish authorities are bound to give notice, under penalty of five-and-twenty roubles for every month's delay. So much bread or corn is then allowed for the infant recruit, which is fetched monthly from the nearest town.

And now for the milder view of this system, which at present buys the public protection at the price of domestic misery. If the recruit be taken early in life with no bonds of wife or children, his prospects may be considered as fair as those of any peasant at home. If he fall beneath an honest and humane officer, fairer still, for he is secure of good maintenance and good clothing. If the individual himself be industrious and careful he may, from the sale of his surplus bread,—for when honestly dealt by he has more per day than he can consume,

—from the sale of his *Schnapps*, or dram, and other extra rations which he receives upon every grand parade, as well as with the addition of small donations in money which accompany these occasions (his pay is nothing, not above eight roubles a-year)—he may from all these sources realise a fund of three or four hundred roubles to retire with; has learnt a trade, has acquired habits of obedience, and is a free man. If the higher classes in Russia could be depended upon for honesty, the soldier's life would be no longer so pitiable.

Under the present untoward combination of outward monotony and inward languor which this season adduces, it requires rather a severe system of drilling to drive such idle recruits as myself to the study of Russian; and Sascha, who at first was so elated with my progress, that in the pride of her heart she knew not which most to extol, her pupil or herself, now sinks into equal despondence at the apathy with which grammars and dictionaries are regarded, blunders the most unjustifiable repeated day by day, and, worse than all, her respectful remonstrances parried by a saucy word which she wonders how I came by. For Sascha keeps a strict watch over any interloper which may have clandestinely intervened, and piques herself as much upon the decorum of her ideas as upon the correctness of her speech. Not unseldom does her zeal for the latter lead to most amusing disputes, for, in the pride of a Russian tongue, a birthright which she possesses so undisputedly here in our household of simple Estonians, that she begins to look upon it in the light of a personal merit, she assumes a dictatorial tone equally upon the right articulation of any French or German word of Russian embezzlement as upon that of any of her own legitimate mouth-fulls. For the Russian language bears upon itself the most direct evidence of the tardiness of the nation in the race of European civilization. Its scientific terms are French, its mechanical terms German, its naval terms English. But what are these after all but the parasitical incrustations round the mouth of a mine of precious ore?—for such may the internal resources of the Russian language be considered. The native Russian may borrow technicalities from others, but morally, feelingly, or imaginatively, he has an infinitely greater variety of terms at his disposal than any of the nations who may consider themselves his creditors.* At once florid and concise—pliable and vigorous, tender and stern;—redundant in imagery, laconic in axiom, graceful in courtesy, strong in argument, soothing in feeling, and tremendous in denunciation, the latent energies of the language are a prophetic guarantee of the destinies of the nation.

The grammar is excessively verbose and intricate, and, though many have essayed, no modern grammarian has yet succeeded in reducing it to a compass of any encouragement to a learner. Articles the Russian grammar has none, but these are amply indemnified by three genders and eight varyingly terminated

* As one instance of their wealth of words, the connexion which we simply designate as brother-in-law, the Russian specifies by four separate terms, distinctly defining the nature of the tie—*Zjat,* or sister's husband; *Schurin,* or wife's brother; *Dever,* or husband's brother; *Svoik,* or wife's sister's husband.

cases, which are brought into active requisition by an unusual abundance of preposition and conjunction. The declension of all parts of speech is highly irregular, the construction of words particularly synthetic. The language is profusely strewn with proverbs, phrases of courtesy, and other Orientalisms which occur in daily use. For instance, every nation has some mode, more or less characteristic, of recommending themselves to the memory of distant friends: the French send friendship; the Germans, greeting; the English, love; the Estonians, health; but with Oriental gravity the Russians, even in the most intimate relations of life, send only a *Poklan*,—literally, an obeisance, or salaam.

With regard to the literature of Russia, it is neither sufficient in volume nor nationality to warrant an opinion. Lomonosoff is the etymologist of the empire; Karamsin, the historian; Pouschkin and Derjavine, the poets; Gretsch and Bestucheff, its prose writers and novelists. Among the collective forty volumes of the latter writer is included a most interesting "*Poyesda vui Reveli,*" or Journey to Reval, presenting the most concise history of the province I have been able to procure. Generally speaking, however, Russian reading is confined to translations of the light French, German, and English works of the day. Our modern novels, including Miss Edgeworth's " Helen," are already in this form.

The picture of English manners which many of our later novels hold up is not always what we ourselves have reason to be satisfied with, while the foreigner, to whom, in his complete ignorance of the relations of English society, such representations are little better than a kind of Chinese puzzle, with a deficiency of pieces which he seeks to supply from his own misfitting stores, produces a caricature still less agreeable to our national pride. For example, that word better felt than defined—that catholic term in good English society,—" the perfect gentleman," is here apprehended only in its outward rank, not in its inward virtue. The only idea a foreigner attaches to the word is that of an empty fop—rich of course, moving in a narrow line of prejudice and conceit, who is equally spoiled at home and ridiculed abroad; while the fact of its being the magical watchword for all that is noble and honourable in public and private life, the bond of honesty, the pledge for liberality, the test of good breeding. the conventional security, stronger than law, between man and man—felt by the noble in mind, paraded by the vulgar, and respected by the degraded,—the fact that the real sense of the word comprehends all this and much more, is as little suspected as believed by the foreigner unacquainted with English life. Let me not be supposed to imply that no foreigner can in his own person represent this term in its utmost meaning; happily the feeling is of universal growth, but Russia is not the land where that national acknowledgment of its influence, which saves so much time and expense, and gives such direct evidence of its existence, is to be found.

It is well that I have fallen thus late in my letter upon a subject which not even the drowsy languor of a Russian April can affect, or a rhapsody upon the perfections of my native land, never seen in brighter colours than when distant from her shores, might usurp the more legitimate vocation of these letters.

It is no less true, however, that "the best patriot is the best cosmopolitan."

LETTER THE FIFTEENTH.

Sudden burst of Spring—Last sledging drive—Thaw in the town and thaw in the country—The *Eisgang*—Inundation—Rapidity of Nature's movements—Green fields and trees—Nightingales without sentiment—Family party—Introduction of a bride elect—Herrmann B.

May 1st.

" Der Sommer ist kommen, die Lerche singt ihr frohes Lied,
 Der Schnee ist zerronnen, das Veilchen lieblich blüht
Est tönen die Lieder so leiblich und schön,
 Ja, Sommer du bist kommen, und laue Lüfte weh'n,
 Ja, Sommer du bist kommen, wie herrlich, oh wie schön!"

THESE must have been the grateful exclamations of some long Russian winter's recluse, for none other, I fancy, can adequately conceive the rapture with which the dawning blessings of summer are hailed. In imitation of Nature's movements every creature seems anxious to throw aside the badges of their long captivity.

Our jingling sledges, our smothering furs and cushions, and our double windows, are now discarded. The cattle have emerged from their various arks of refuge, and with their stiff winter limbs are creeping slowly about, snuffing the brown and yet lifeless grass. The peasants have cast aside their greasy sheepkins, and are pattering about with bare legs. The tender children of the family, whose bleached cheeks have mutely pleaded against the tardiness of spring, and who have in vain sought to substitute the freedom of outer exercise by indefatigable chasings through the house's great thoroughfare, are turned out on to the drier heights, with round summer hats and lighter garments, enjoying the warmth of a spring which to them seems the first. While we, like them, for simple pleasures make happy children of us all, revel in the luxury of breathing a softer air, of turning our cheek without fear of a smite, of setting our foot on mud, puddle, black ice, wet stones—on anything, in short, rather than on the beautiful smooth white surface which, like an over-perfect person, has left deeper impression of its monotony than of its beauty.

Our last sledging drive over a morass was a *Strapazz*, or mad freak, not rashly to be renewed; and, like the Prince in the Persian tale, whose spotless mind and rapid speed carried him safe over the slender arch of crystal, while the fair lady pursuing, with foot less light than her reputation, dropped instantly through, we seemed to owe our safety across our crystal plain as much to the winged speed of our horses as to any particular purity of conscience. It was a necessary visit which called us out, and our coachman, a very dare-devil of a Russian, emboldened by long luck, and versed in every track, guaranteed, if we went and returned before the full warmth of the day had contributed to the work of destruction, to take us safe across. So off we set, " splash, splash, across the sea," through a foot deep of water standing upon the yet unbroken bed of ice, while the great cattle-dogs who followed at a labouring gallop, and were tempted from the track by some delicious half-thawed piece of putrefaction, the relic of the preceding autumn, had many a spluttering immersion.

I have had the opportunity of witnessing the revolution of thaw both in country and town. In the former it is sublime—in the latter ridiculous. In Reval it made many attempts before the final breaking up, thawing rapidly in the day and freezing hard at night, till a few serious falls made the householders look about them, and, by the time the thaw was fairly set in, sand was strewed plentifully about the streets. One evening, not aware in our equably warm rooms of the change of atmosphere, we left our house to proceed to that of a friend not six doors removed—being previously well provided with Indian rubber caloshes, the worst conductors in the world on slippery roads. At our first step of descent from the house, whose elevated situation has been described, our feet were taken most unaccountably from beneath us, and still faithfully hand-in-hand, we performed a *glissade* of considerable length, being only stopped by a ledge in the pavement upon the *place* below. The difficulty now was to rise, for all beneath and around was as polished glass, and tottering, slipping, and laughing we stood leaning upon a friendly lamp-post, able neither to proceed backwards nor forwards—our friend's lighted windows in front, our own behind, both looking all the more tempting because so utterly unattainable. A few solitary sledges passed us in the centre of the square, and, regardless of what type of Estonian decorum they might envelope, we hailed the fur mantles seated within, but either not hearing, or not heeding, they passed on one after the other to the castle of the governor, which was illuminated for a *soirée*, and we were left clinging to our lantern, which emitted a feeble glimmer over our heads,—for gas is too "new a light" for Reval,—and repeated its rays in the watery ice beneath our feet. At length a sturdy Russian sailor came up, trudging along in his rough boots as safe as a fly on a pane of glass, and to him we applied: "*Kudi vui velite, Sudarina?*" or "whither do you desire, Signora?" Half ashamed we pointed back to our own door, hardly above a long arm's reach from us, for all thoughts of proceeding further on these terms were abandoned. The sailor looked at us in some doubt as to our sanity, but with Russian courtesy, giving a hand to each, and setting his feet like a Colossus of Rhodes, he hauled us up, acknowledging at our repeated backslidings, "*Verno, otchen gliska!*"—Truly, very slippery!

This was, however, our last dilemma, for now, as if anxious to retrieve its delay, the thaw advanced in such rapid strides that it required, if not more inducement without doors, at all events less happiness than we possessed within, to venture into the streets at all.

It must be remembered that the towns here, like the state of society, have no drains. Therefore the Dome, which, from its natural position, offers the utmost facility for drainage, here simply pours its tribute of dirty ice water with a kind of stepmother love into the town below. For several days the householders contemplate with perfect equanimity the spectacle of the whole *Douglasberg* and *Domberg* one stream of running water, while deep puddles of a black merging into an orange hue settle at the foundations of their houses, particularly embosoming the house door, and ooze into their cellar grates. Choice of footing there is none, and gentlemen turn up their trousers, and ladies tuck up their petticoats, and, in lieu of these, drabble the corners of their cloaks, and the tails of their boas; and go about stepping from Scylla to Charybdis, and complaining that their houses are *damp*. And if two bosom friends chance to start on opposite sides of the street, there they must remain, were their hearts to break. With gentlemen no such dilemma exists, they being just as cordial on bad roads as on good ones. And now the sun darts a fiercer ray, and the thaw increases, and the roofs bring their tribute, and pour and patter down upon sealskin caps, or pink satin bonnets, or into baskets of white bread, or hot *brei* puddings; and these being past, bore deep holes in the yet unmelted ice pavement, and lay bare the rough old stones beneath: and then little puddles join their forces to great puddles; and the *Domberg* stream widens and deepens, and goes babbling along as if delighted with the novelty.

At length the aristocratic count, who all this time has sat upstairs in his dressing-gown, smoking his long pipe, not supposed in the nobility of his heart to know what the vulgar elements are about, issues from his house door, delightfully situated on the very margin of the new stream, himself dressed *à quatre épingles*, and fully bent on calling upon the governor. At the first step he flounders above his caloshes —looking bewildered about him, he catches the eye of an elderly maiden lady at her window opposite, courteously takes off his hat, and down come a volley of drops on his bare head. This comes of a man's walking whose ancestral papers are falling to pieces with mere age: so he recrosses his threshold, not knowing exactly who or what to find fault with, orders his carriage and four to take him a hundred yards, and sends out a couple of men-servants to cut a channel as far as his boundary extends.

And the water follows their strokes, and splashes them to the ears, and runs merrily past the count's house to spread itself in a fertilising stream over the market-place.

Here again it enjoys perfect liberty of conscience, undermining every last morsel of firm ice, filling the cellars with a dirty mixture, and the houses with a dirty smell; while all the filth of the preceding autumn—all the various souvenirs which a merciful winter had rendered innoxious both to eye and nose, now assault both organs, and go swimming about, and doubtless take refuge in the cellars also. Then, one after another, the householders, zealous to shut the door after the steed is stolen, cut drains before their houses, and the streets and *places* of the Dom are divided into patchwork canals, and old *Coya Mutters,* or portresses, assist all remote puddles with worn-out brooms, and the whole collection sooner or later finds its way to the town beneath, where we forbear to follow it.

Such is the history of a town thaw—but the apotheosis of the country is very different.

Here the soft hand of spring imperceptibly withdraws the bolts and bars of winter, while the earth, like a drowsy child 'twixt sleeping and waking, flings off one wrapper after another and opes its heavy lids in showers of sweet rivulets. And the snow disappears, and the brown earth peeps almost dry from beneath; and you wonder where all the mountains of moisture are gone. But wait—the rivers are still locked, and though a strong current is pouring on their surface, yet, from the high bridge, the green ice is still seen deep below, firm as a rock—and dogs go splashing over in the old track, and peasants with their horses venture long after it seems prudent. At length a sound like distant thunder, or the crashing of a forest, meets your ear, and the words "*D'er Eisgang, der Eisgang!*" pass from mouth to mouth, and those who would witness this northern scene hurry out to the old stone bridge, and are obliged to take a circuitous route, for the waters have risen ankle deep—and then another crash, and you double your pace, regardless of wet feet, and are startled at the change which a few hours have produced. On the one side, close besetting the bridge, and high up the banks, lies a field of ice lifting the waters before it, and spreading them over the country; while huge masses flounder and swing against one another with loud reports, and heave up their green transparent edges, full six feet thick, with a majestic motion; and all these press heavily upon the bridge, which trembles at every stroke, and stands like a living thing labouring and gasping for breath through the small apertures of the almost choked arches. On the other side the river is free of ice, and a furious stream, as if all the imprisoned waters of Russia were let loose, is dashing down, bearing with it some huge leviathan of semi-transparent crystal, and curdling its waters about it, till this again is stopped by another field of ice lower down.

The waters were rising every minute—night was approaching, and the beautiful old bridge gave us great alarm, when a party of peasants, fresh from their supper at the *Hof*, and cheered with brandy, arrived to relieve it. Each was

Sheep Stable.

armed with a long pole with an iron point, and flying down the piles and on to the ice itself, began hacking at the sides of the foremost monster, till, impelled by the current beneath, it could fit and grind itself through the bridge and gallop down to thunder against its comrades below. The men were utterly fearless, giving a keen sense of adventure to their dangerous task which riveted us to the spot; some of the most daring standing and leaning with their whole weight over the bed of the torrent upon the very mass they were hewing off, till the slow swing which preceded the final plunge made them fly to the piles for safety. Some fragments were doubly hard with imbedded stones and pieces of timber, and no sooner was one enemy despatched than another succeeded; and although bodies of men continued relieving each other all night, the bridge sustained such damage as could not be repaired. All was over in twelve hours, but meanwhile " the waters prevailed exceedingly upon the earth," and every hill and building stood insulated.

Such was the picture of our life a fortnight

ago, since when a still more striking change, if possible, has come over the face of things. The earth, which so late emerged from her winter garb, is now clad in the liveliest livery; while every tree and shrub have hastily changed their dresses in Nature's vast greenroom, and stand all ready for the summer's short act. Nowhere is Nature's hocus-pocus carried on so wonderfully—nowhere her scene-shifting so inconceivably rapid. You may literally see her movements. I have watched the bird's-cherry at my window. Two days ago, and it was still the same dried up spectre, whose every form, during the long winter, the vacant eye had studiously examined while the thoughts were far distant—yesterday, like the painter's Daphne, it was sprouting out at every finger, and to-day it has shaken out its whole complement of leaves, and is throwing a verdant twilight over my darkened room. The whole air is full of the soft stirring sounds of the swollen buds snapping and cracking into life, and impregnated with the perfume of the fresh, oily leaves. The waters are full and clear—the skies blue and serene—night and day are fast blending into one continuous stream of soft light, and this our new existence is one perpetual feast. Oh winter! where is thy victory? The resurrection of spring speaks volumes.

This is the time for giving and receiving visits, and our neighbours, who thaw with the season, are now seen driving about, not in sledges, but in their high-wheeled carriages;—the only exchange of the spring we are inclined to regret—taking their meals, in defiance of swarms of gnats and flies, upon their long-neglected balconies, and listening to the nightingales whose gurgling throats are heard incessant, day and night, till our daintier ears rebel at this surfeit of sweet sounds. For Philomel, instead of pouring her plaint to the night, heard only by those whom kindred miseries forbid to sleep, here boldly takes her station by broad sunshine, and like some persons whose incorrigible thirst for pity leads them to overlook all the decencies of sorrow, parades her griefs, equally visibly as audibly, to all who will listen; in vain endeavouring to overpower the peals of a rival sufferer perched on an opposite tree. How truly has Portia said,

> "The nightingale, if she should sing by day,
> When every goose is cackling, would be thought
> No better a musician than the wren."

Here this bird of sorrow loses all her sentiment.

The gardeners are now occupied in calling the gardens into existence, for at the commencement of winter every plant is taken up and consigned to its winter cellar, not to resume its station till summer appears; and the families are wandering about, scanning the grounds as fondly as if returned to some long-withheld inheritance. Truly we might take a lesson from this frugal northern people how to prize the gifts of Nature.

Here every species of pleasure-ground goes under the grand denomination of a *park*, and it is impossible to convince those worthy foreigners that their wild meadow and forest scenery approaches much nearer the reality, and indeed requires no alteration in many instances beyond that of neatness; though other parts of their heathy and morassy landscape would lose in beauty by cultivation.

At one house we found every degree of relationship gathered together for the ceremony of introduction to a young lady just engaged to the eldest son. We should think such matters better honoured in the breach than in the observance, but here the *Braut*, a silent poke-headed girl, went passively through the ordeal; the mistress of the family presenting her to each as " *meine Schwiegertochter,*" my daughter-in-law—for in Estonia, let the period of marriage be ever so distant, the nearest titles of relationship are adopted by anticipation. By this means a single lady, if she prove rather changeable, may provide herself with a large circle of connexions before she be burdened with a husband. Among the party was a young Russian *Garde Officier*, then enjoying his year of absence from the service—one of the many privileges attending the acquisition of an epaulette,—though no release from the uniform is allowed; and who evidently made the most of his holiday by not opening his lips, or changing his position more than was absolutely necessary: so that a little sketch of combined Russian drilling and German phlegma was made without his being in any way accessary to the fact. But "*stille Wasser sind tief,*" and though Herrmann B. made his large brown eyes do all the work for his tongue, yet I suspect there was more behind them than his more talkative companions could boast. Lively conversation, however, is not the favourite bosom sin of an Estonian gentleman, at least not more than can be conveniently combined with the paramount discussion of a pipe, to which, after the novelty of the *Braut* had subsided, they all resorted.

LETTER THE SIXTEENTH.

Early rising—Departure on a journey—Drive through a wild country—Diversities of taste in the situation of a residence — A *Krug* — Rosenthal — Boulder stones — Castle Lode, and the unfortunate Princess of Wirtemberg—A very hard bed—Leal—An accumulation of annoyances—The Wieck, and its seashore riches—Baron Ungern Sternberg—Count and Countess ———, and their seat at Linden—Anecdote of Peter the Great and his friend Menschikoff—The Castle of Habsal—Dagen girl—Odd collections—Riesenberg and the Baroness S.

Our journey to . . . commenced on the 10th of June. At four in the morning we awoke to a sky cool as night and bright as noon, but human nature was not the less sleepy, and Sascha had alternately repeated in tones of progressive loudness "It is four of the clock—it is the fifth hour," and blurted out various adjurations in Russian, which, as they would infallibly have puzzled her *Barishna*, or lady, when wide awake, she inversely reasoned would effectually arouse her when half asleep, before she could be prevailed upon to stir. Oh this getting up! what a daily torment is it!—watchings and vigils are nothing in comparison! In vain would we run away from our sins; your sound morning sleepers are just as incorrigible in the full uncurtained blaze of a Russian June, as in the drowsy candlelight of a London November. But who calls the callers? Here we will change the subject.

Then came the hasty breakfast—the final closing of the great *Speise Korb*, or provision basket, on which all hopes of good cheer in this country depend—the last injunctions to the household—the last kisses to children, and off we set in an open barouche and four, well settled down in a comfortable carriage-position, and well disposed to enjoy our journey, or rather that luxurious, untiring converse of two individuals, near and dear, who have spent all life's youth together and gathered much of life's experience apart. Nor was this delicious tête à-tête through moist plains and hazy woods whose boughs swept our carriage, and whose murmurs scarce before mingled with the lisping sounds of English, likely to be interrupted: for on his box sat Mart, the Estonian coachman, and before us sat Sascha, the Russian maid, and my dear companion spoke no Russian, and I no Estonian, and the two servants were equally mute to each other, so that of our quartet only two could exchange speech together, and that in three languages alternately.

It was a strange but sweet drive through this wild country, of which we seemed the only passing tenants,—occasionally rousing ourselves from some mutual reminiscence of girlhood's fancied grief, or soberer relation of womanhood's real sorrow, from dreams and scenes only of the past,—for those who love deeply and soon must part care not for the future,—to gaze at some untutored beauty in the landscape, which each equally admired, or some tasteless freak of man which both equally laughed at. This, however, does not apply to the country houses, which, with the exception of the wooden ones, are generally built with taste, and often with magnificence, but to the choice of a position, where, it is true, the good Estonians do not shine. Often in the course of our journey did the road lead us through winding avenues of majestic trees, or parky ground laid out by Nature's hand, where the eye involuntarily sought the mansion of the proprietor—but sought in vain: for if one estate be more plentifully gifted with the beauties of wood and cliff, stream or lake, than another, there you may be sure the mansion, splendid in itself, is planted in some industriously picked corner, just where none of these are visible. To approach a house through shadeless corn-fields is the thing in Estonia; and as for a view, they prefer that of their own farming buildings, not always so ornamental as the sheep-stable we have portrayed, to anything Nature can offer. Listen to that pretty woman who sits bolt upright on that hard chair: she is describing an estate her husband has lately purchased. "The house stands on a hill—beneath it a valley with a beautiful——" what? a beautiful stream? by no means: a beautiful forest? neither; but "*une belle étable,*" and that with a red-tiled roof.

But to return to our pleasant drive. Mankind now began to emerge—peasants, with files of carts laden with brandy or milk, turned off for the carriage of the *Sachsa*, as they still designate their Teutonic-descended masters—little peasant children with no further incumbrance than a shift, and heads of hair like shaggy poodle dogs, darted from a thicket to open a gate, while here a woman toiled at the plough, and a man smoked and looked on, and there a man was brutally beating a girl, whilst women stood by with unconcern. And in this latter case we could not resist interference, and Mart delivered a most impressive admonition from his mistress's lips in improved Estonian, which was received sulkily, and like most temporary relief I dare say did its object more harm than good.

By eight o'clock the sun had acquired more heat than was agreeable to bear, and by ten it was insupportable, and our spirited horses hung their heads, and only languidly repelled the attacks of the great flies, big as cockchafers, called here *Bremsen*, which followed them in flights,—sometimes blundering into the carriage, to the great interruption of all romantic reminiscences. Under these circumstances the roof of the great *Krug* which reared itself in the distance was rather a more welcome sight than usual—a building so denuded of every comfort, that it is difficult to conceive how a travelling people like the Estonians, who are always staging from one great house to another, and traverse thousands of wersts in a year within the bounds of their own province, have not encouraged better accommodations. These *Krugs* are at once the public-houses of the peasantry, and the only inns of the gentler traveller—immense erections, often very picturesque without, and particularly picturesque within also!—of which there are one or more on every estate, and whence a decent revenue is derived from the sale of brandy and beer. Those Krugs whose position on a high

Estonian Krug

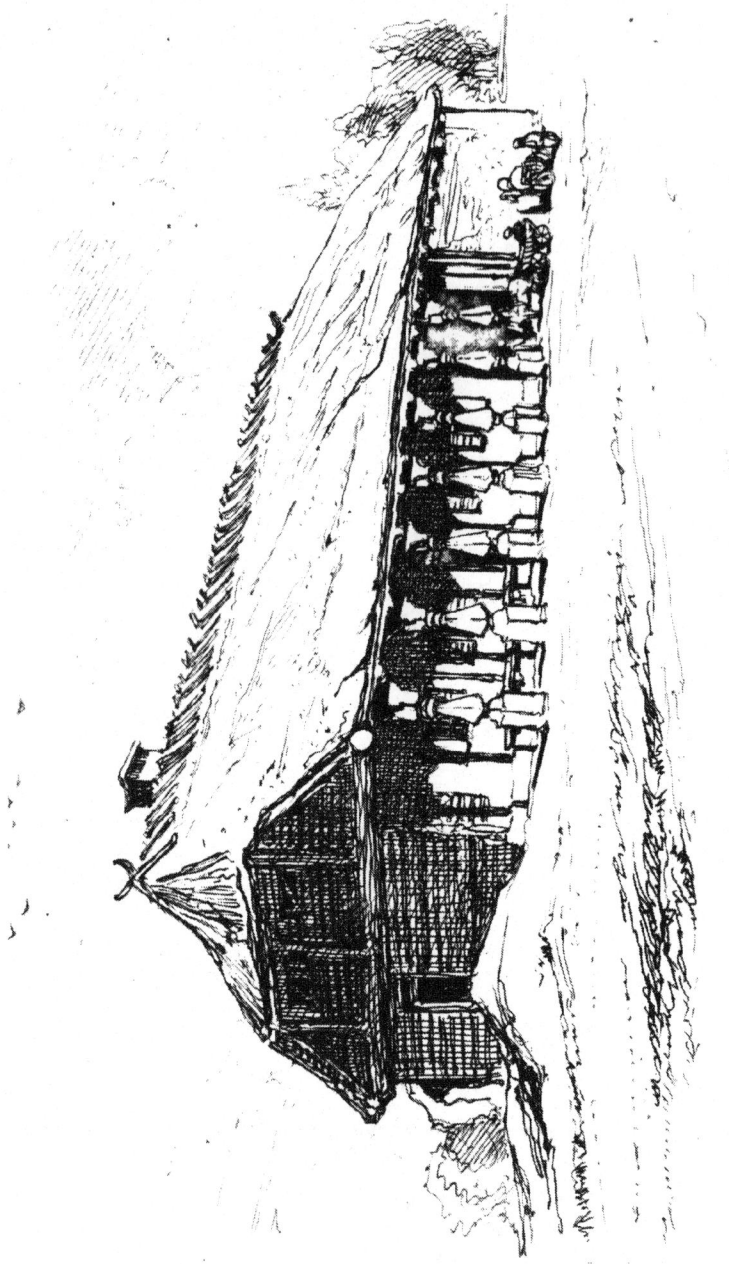

road leads them to expect company of a better sort are kept by Germans, speaking most ungrammatical German, with all the pretensions of a better class, and the squalidness of the very lowest. Here a room or two is allotted to the carriage traveller, where you are expected to bring your own provisions to spread the filthy table, and your own cushions to fill the wretched bedstead. After a hearty inroad into our *Speise Korb*, and a short nap upon a bench so narrow that the first uneasy start threatened to fling the sleeper on the floor, but which offered the advantage of the least possible contact with surrounding objects, we turned out into Nature's vast hostelry, leaving Sascha and Mart to converse with their eyes.

Before us was a handsome country house, called *Rosenthal*, belonging to a proprietor of the same name, surrounded with gardens of unusual beauty, which, though utter strangers, we received a courteous invitation to explore, and where, with sketch-book in hand, and a sweet voice at my side, more than the miseries of an Estonian Krug would soon have been forgotten. The country was very fertile—enormous fields of waving corn, some of them above a hundred acres in extent, hemmed in with lofty woods, and dotted with those stones which form a peculiar feature in an Estonian landscape. These are blocks of granite, varying in size from huge masses, big as houses, of every picturesque form and colour, to such as one man could lift, which lie strewed in myriads upon the surface of this country, to which they are not indigenous,—especially lining the sea-coast,—and doubtless have been rent in some convulsion of nature from the opposite granite shores of Finland. I was laughed at for calling them *rocks*, though, if size be a qualification for that title, many deserve it. Here they are called, concurring in name as well as in meaning with our *boulder* stones, *Bulla Steine*. To pick the fields clean of these foreigners to the soil would be impossible, but the smaller ones are culled off for fences, and other purposes of building.

By this time the horses had enjoyed their necessary rest, and we resumed our carriage posi-

Castle Lode

tion,—the only comfortable one to be had,—and passing through many pretty estates and fields of wheat, here a rare sight, came in view of the towers of Castle Lode about seven in the evening. Here another Krug, rather less comfortless than the Rosenthal one, received us—having the addition of a tallow-besprinkled billiard table to the other stated furniture. But the old castle had sufficient interest to render the evening agreeable. It is a fine building with massive towers, enclosing a courtyard, with the inscription " Albertus de Buxhoveden Episcopus, renovavit 1435," and entered by a massive bridge and gateway over a moat. Altogether a most picturesque spot, with fine old trees and majestic expanse of water;—nothing wanted but more ruin or more repair.* Its history dates from the earliest episcopal times in Estonia, being mentioned as a bishop's castle as early as the thirteenth century. It sustained many sieges,

* These words seem ill-fated, for a few months subsequent to our visit this castle was reduced by fire to a state of ruin. A sketch of it in this condition has been preferred to one taken previously.

and all the wear and tear of a country so long divided within itself and contended for by others, and under Peter the Great became crown property, being appropriated as a prison for state offences. The last inmate in this capacity was a Princess of Wirtemberg, whose fate has given a horrible interest to its walls. She was confined here by Catherine II.; some say for having divulged a state secret, others for having attracted the notice of her son Paul. Be this as it may, she was young and very beautiful—was at first lodged here with the retinue and distinction befitting her rank, and is still remembered by some of the oldest noblemen in the province as having entertained them with much grace, and condescended to join in the waltz, where her personal charms and womanly coquetry, joined to the romance of her misfortunes and high rank, gained her many manly hearts. But like a royal predecessor in history, her charms proved her destruction. To her infinite wretchedness, they gained the attention of General Pohlmann, who had the charge of the beautiful prisoner. Under divers pretences her attendants were diminished, her liberty curtailed, and her keeper proved himself a villain. The sequel to this was her death under most heart-rending circumstances, being left like a second Genofeva utterly unassisted and uncared for at the time of giving birth to an infant, of which she was not delivered, and which perished with her. Her corpse was put into a cellar of the castle—all inquiry stifled upon the spot, and, being obnoxious to Catherine, no appeal to her justice was made. Nothing was done in Paul's time, nor in Alexander's, nor in short till a few years back, when the Prince of Oldenburg, nearly related to the deceased, came expressly to Castle Lode. Owing to the quality of the atmosphere the body was found in a state of preservation, which left no doubt as to the cause of her death, and was decently interred in the church of Goldenbeck, close by.

We lingered about the spot and saw happy children's faces gleaming from those rooms which this last hapless prisoner had inhabited, and returning to our Krug ordered clean hay into our empty bedsteads, and disposed ourselves to rest. But the shade of the Princess of Wirtemberg haunted our minds; and as for our bodies, never did I know how much it required to make a bed soft before. Sleep without rest is worse than no sleep at all, nor could all the drowsiness in the world dull the intolerable aching of our bones as we turned from side to side on those hard planks. At length, persuading ourselves that it would be better for man and horse to avoid the heat of the day, we roused Mart from his softer lair beside his steeds, who rose, like a willing, gentle Estonian, without a murmur, and Sascha from her elbows on the table, whose little Tartar eyes could hardly open at all, and leaving our bed to hardier-nursed travellers, we dozed on in the carriage; waking up as we splashed through a wide stream, and then dozing again till we reached Leal at five. This place, which consists of little more than a long street of wretched houses, is called, *par excellence, das Fleck* Leal;—literally *the spot* Leal,—and spot, hole, nest, call it what they will, never was there such a detestable abode seen. We stopped at a Krug, where not a creature was stirring, and, after knocking in vain, opened a door, when a scene presented itself which beggars all description. I have portrayed to you the day aspect of a Volks Stube—we now saw the night one. About twenty creatures were lying on stove, floor, and table—old and young—boys and girls —higgledy-piggledy— the atmosphere at least 100°, and thick and reeking from this human hecatomb. In the centre of the floor lay a wayworn soldier with his martial cloak around him, the only decent figure of the party, which, with the exception of an old hag, who came forward in a state which made us retreat, slept on unconcerned at our entrance. Never was poor humanity seen under a more disgusting aspect. In vain did Sascha stand behind with Speise Korb on arm—no place was clean enough to receive it; and as for ourselves, we had been better off in an English pigsty. So out we sallied, tired, hungry, chilly, and dirty, and in the very worst of all possible humours with the *Fleck* and all its inhabitants, and sat down in the churchyard to while away time. The *Fleck*, however, boasts a history—has fragments of a castle and monastery still standing—has been besieged over and over again, and almost burnt down several times—I heartily wish it had been so quite. After studying all the inscriptions in the churchyard, alternately German and Estonian, with here and there a stray Swedish memento, and looking at our watches to hurry time in vain, we returned to our carriage, where poor tired Sascha was enjoying a short oblivion from her woes. Rather than disturb her, we bethought ourselves to try an Estonian Krug close by, for those incarnations of nastiness who had assailed us upon our arrival were Germans, and would have scorned to be confounded with the peasantry; and here we found, though no great accommodation, yet a clean table and chair in the hostess's room—a brisk, handsome creature, whom we disturbed from her spinning-wheel at the side of her sleeping child, and who soon took her place in my sketch-book.

From Leal we passed through a country uninteresting with the exception of an oak-wood of great age and beauty—a sight of uncommon occurrence—and blocks of granite of immense size which towered above the cornfields, and by ten o'clock reached our journey's end.

We were now in the portion of that province called the *Wieck*; Estonia having been from the earliest times divided into four districts, entitled the Wieck, East and South Harrien, Jerwen, and Wierland, each of which has advantages of some kind or other, as the old song celebrates:—

> "In dem Wieck, da wird man rieck;
> "In Harrien, da wohnen die Karrien;
> "In Wierland, ist gut Bierland;
> "In Jerwen möcht ich leben und sterben."

One drawback, however, to the wealth of the Wieck is a most monotonous country, with large sandy and morassy tracts, but highly fertile under cultivation, which both the priests and knights no doubt discovered, for this district appears to have been more particularly their residence. Lying also along the coast of the Baltic, here excessively dangerous to navigators, the shattered fortunes of a Wieck seigneur are not unseldom repaired by *reiche Strandungen,* literally rich strandings, which the spring and autumn winds, in their fury up and down this narrow sea, throw on their shores. Not long ago one of these gentlemen had a cargo of the best Champagne wafted to his feet, just as he was sounding the contents of his cellar in preparation for the marriage feasting of his adopted daughter.

It is a barbarous custom this strand-right, but civilization is not sufficiently advanced here to dispense with it, and fewer lives would be saved if this bribe to cupidity were not held out. That period of cruelty when false lights were hung out to entangle ships is passed away with the fate of the notorious Baron Ungern Sternberg, who from his own house, situated on a high part of the island of Dagen, where he lived in undisputed authority, displayed a light which misled many a mariner. This continued unnoticed, for he was powerful in wealth and influence, till the disappearance of a ship's captain, who was found dead in his room: the existence of goods to a large extent under the floors of the house, and other concurring circumstances, led to his apprehension. His family, one of the highest in the province, urged him to fly, but he was fearless to the last. Some of his contemporaries still remember his trial, which took place thirty-two years back, when he appeared before the Landräthe, his equals, in the garb of a peasant, with chains on hands and feet, and was condemned to Siberia, but not to the mines. His name was struck off the roll of nobility, but his children's left untouched. Some think him hardly done by, and his family stands high as ever; and, if they have not inherited the crimes, they have at all events the daring courage, enterprise, shrewd sense, and sparkling wit of their pirate ancestor. I have been told by an English seaman that the sensation of this affair extended even to England, and that placards were seen in the streets of London—"Beware of Ungern Sternberg, the Sea Robber,"—as a warning to sailors.

At two days' end, having accomplished a

visit of too serious and private an import to be commented upon here, we resumed our journey, and took the road for the seat of Count ——, at Linden, near Habsal. Here, unless the traveller know the Estonian as well as the German name of an estate, he is no nearer the object of his search; and, doubtful of our road, we had to inquire for the *Ungere Mois*, or Ungern estate, Linden having formerly belonged to this family. This is one of those houses which that said refinement which lieth not in the purse, and which both the Count and his beautiful Countess cordially agree in maintaining, has filled with those numerous, nameless little comforts which cost little beyond the thought. Linden is one of the most delightful residences I have seen, but at the same time our Count is one whose presence would enliven the four bare walls of an Estonian Krug. Wit without effort, kindness without display, nobility as much by nature as descent, and a life of adventure, combine to make him one of the most charming specimens of aristocratic mankind, whether seen in Estonia or England

This estate lies directly on the coast, the passing vessels visible from the drawing-room windows, and has been immortalized by the presence of Peter the Great, who visited it in his peregrinations along the shores of the Baltic for the purpose of ascertaining the best position for his future capital. The Zar and his inseparable friend Menschikoff were here entertained in fear and trembling by a pretty widow, Countess Steenbock, née Baroness Ungern, whose feelings lay with her late sovereign Charles XII. of Sweden. Nevertheless Peter felt very well disposed towards his pretty hostess, but Menschikoff was on the alert to catch up anything that could at once demonstrate her lukewarmness and his loyalty. Occasion for this soon presented itself at dinner upon the Zar's health being given by the Countess, when Menschikoff's wary eye quickly observed that the goblet whereout she drank was decorated with the royal arms of Sweden, and thundered out a remonstrance in the style of the day, doubtless more loyal than gentle. The Countess said nothing, but a tear, as our host assures us, stood in her beautiful eye, and Peter, whose heart could better brook torrents of men's blood than one pearly drop from pretty woman, thundered back upon his High Admiral all the opprobrious epithets he could remember, desiring him to fall in love with her that moment and make her his wife for an atonement. Of course Menschikoff did as he was bid, but the Countess's tears flowed faster and faster, for she thought no fate so horrible as that of being a Russian's wife, and, relying on the generosity of a discarded lover, more to be trusted, it is true, than a favoured one, avowed herself the betrothed of her cousin Hans Rosen, who lived on the island of Dagen, just opposite her windows. So Menschikoff's ardour as suddenly cooled, and Baron Rosen took the widow at her word, and from their descendants our fascinating Count inherited the estate of Linden.

From Linden we visited Habsal, a small sea-port-town which at one time enjoyed considerable importance, but whose chief attraction now consists in bathing-houses in summer, and the magnificent remains of the castle, formerly the residence of the Bishops of Habsal. From the magnitude of the ruins, this appears to have been an episcopal castle of uncommon splendour. The church, with cloisters and chapel adjoining, as well as part of the refectory, a tower, and other portions, are still standing, and are surrounded by embankments and a massive wall of great beauty, secured at intervals by turreted towers: outside of these is a garden with fruit-trees venerable as the ruin, with a moat beyond surrounding that portion which the sea does not protect. Habsal shared all the vicissitudes of Estonia,—was plundered by the infuriated peasantry, who made the Wieck especially the theatre of their excesses, and more than once bartered with the neighbouring castles of Leal and Lode for gold.

Count —— is now erecting and adorning a mansion which has the rare view of a fine Gothic castle on the right, and the waves of the Baltic on the left, and promises to be as comfortable within as it is magnificent without. He is possessed of large property, including quarries of a fine quality of stone, with which a contract has recently been made to repave Petersburg, and is the encourager of all ingenuity in the peasants, and the promoter of labour for wages. Large estates on the island of Dagen are also his. The peasantry there have a distinct costume, and amongst his household was a Dagen girl, who was handed blushing into the drawing-room for us to examine her accoutrements. The head-dress was a circular plait of hair, braided with a red cloth roll, which fastened behind, and hung down in long ends tipped with gold fringe. The dress was merely a linen shift, high to the throat, and half-leg long, crimped from top to bottom—the linen being soaked with as much strong starch as it can hold, crimped with long laths of wood, and then put into the oven to dry, whence it issues stiff and hard as a board. How the Dagen ladies manage to sit down in this case of iron is more than I can say, since we did not see this evolution performed. The belt, however, is the chief curiosity, being made of broad black leather, studded with massive brass heads, with a second hanging belt in military guise, whence a knife in a silver case is suspended, and which fastens behind with a fringe of brass chains. High-heeled shoes and red stockings completed the attire, and altogether a prettier bandit maiden never was seen.

Linden is stored with all the curiosities which the combined taste and humour of our host has collected. Here may be seen beautifully carved Gothic furniture, and in a conspicuous place the painted figure-head of an English vessel;—fine old armour, inlaid firelocks, and a rapier which a middle-sized man must mount a chair to unsheath;—good pictures of ancestors, and one of a burning town where the moon is introduced as foreground;—collections of snuff-boxes, &c., and vaious relics of his grandsire the King of Sweden; and lastly, a collection of a peculiar kind of snuff-box, which the Count flattered himself not even one of our own *bizarres* countrymen would have thought of making; so, with the particular sparkle of the eye and compression of lip which always preceded an act or saying which made everybody laugh but himself, he opened a drawer where lay in sad inactivity—a whole collection of—snuffers. There were snuffers *couchant*, and snuffers *rampant*—snuffers which no one could have guessed to be snuffers, and yet which looked like nothing else in art or nature— Russian snuffers fine with gilding, but which rattled and let out the snuff—a curious German contrivance which required three hands, and a Chinese one with a trigger to pull, producing a concussion which generally snuffed the candle—out;—and lastly, as a satire upon the whole, there was a genuine Birmingham pair—light, bright, and plain—which with one gentle click did the work of all the party.

What a pity it is that Count ―― has no children to inherit his fine property and finer disposition! He is now petitioning the Emperor for leave to legate both title and estates to a sister's son; but come what may, there will never be such another Count ―― as the present. Two happy days were here snatched from time, and when the farewell hour arrived we forgot how recent had been our knowledge of each other, and only feared the future might never reunite those whom fate had placed so far asunder. And again a tear stood in the eye of the beautiful hostess of Linden, and our host looked strenuously towards his own feet— the neatest, by the way, in the world—and attempted some humorous demonstrations of the fidelity of manly memories, and the faithlessness of feminine: but it would not do; and we were worse than either. It is pleasant to rove through the world, but it is hard to part from those who gratuitously receive the stranger as the friend.

We left Linden at an unusual hour—our time was scarce and our energies plentiful, so we enjoyed our friends' society till midnight, and set off in the short twilight. Our horses had been sent forward about twenty miles, it being the conventional courtesy in this country for the host to give you his own horses for the first stage, and for the hostess to replenish your Speise Korb with the best from her table. Repassing Lode, we took a different route, and halted a few hours at Riesenberg, the seat of Baron S., and one of the most magnificent houses to be found here or in any country. The Baroness S. is a perfect Flora in taste, which with her, from the peculiar art she possesses of heightening Nature's beauty by a certain poetry of arrangement, amounts to real genius. Not only do her gardens and grounds bloom beneath her hands, but she has taught her flowers to spring from one pillar to another of her beautiful saloon, nestling themselves in rich clusters amongst the architectural ornaments, and hanging above like censers of rich perfumes, till, with the little blonde Cupids, whom she has also contrived to rear in profusion, sporting on the parquête floor beneath, a prettier scene can hardly be imagined.

Nothing can exceed the hospitality of the Estonians. Servants, horses, all are equally entertained, and the traveller sent rejoicing on his way, never to forget obligations so unostentatiously bestowed. From Riesenberg we commenced our last stage homeward, and leaning back with tired langour resumed that intimate language of affection, that sweet flow of uttered thought, which "pours from hearts

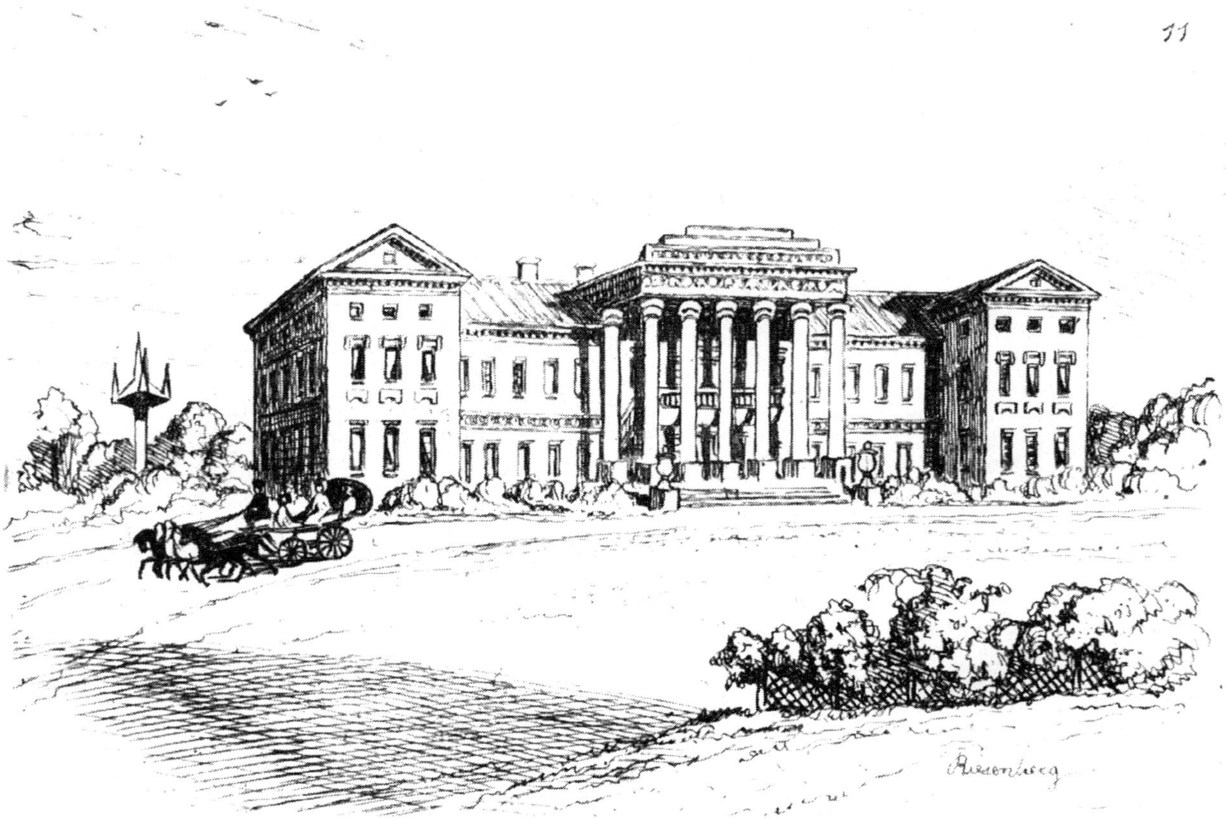
Riesenberg

by nature matched." And, low in the heavens, the bright orb of day, which had attended us in cloudless splendour from two in the morning—the steps of Aurora being at this season here followed by at least twenty rosy hours—streamed cool and subdued through groves of slender-stemmed trees, reminding us at every instant of Turner's matchless productions, (for who like him has ever realised the truth of a sunny day, the golden fields, the fleecy clouds, and countless fluttering, glittering leaves?) and at last sunk to his short rest again before we reached ours.

LETTER THE SEVENTEENTH.

Bathing life at Reval—Custom-house troubles extraordinary—Voyage across the Gulf—Union of various nations—Approach to Helsingforst—A ball—Baroness K.—Shopping propensities of lady passengers—Granite beauties of Helsingforst—The Observatory—The Botanical Garden—An eventful dinner—Sweaborg—The Scheeren—Symptoms of smuggling—Return to Reval.

We have resumed our life in Reval, the population of which is now swelled with hundreds of bathing guests—chiefly Petersburgians, who, enervated by the long winter's confinement and dissipation, imbibe fresh life both from the air and water of this pretty bay; and Germans, Russian bred, who are glad to renew recollections of their fatherland and mother-tongue at so short a distance. The Pyroskaffs between Reval and Petersburg are constantly plying, so overladen with passengers as greatly to neutral-

View from the Schaan Bastion Bund

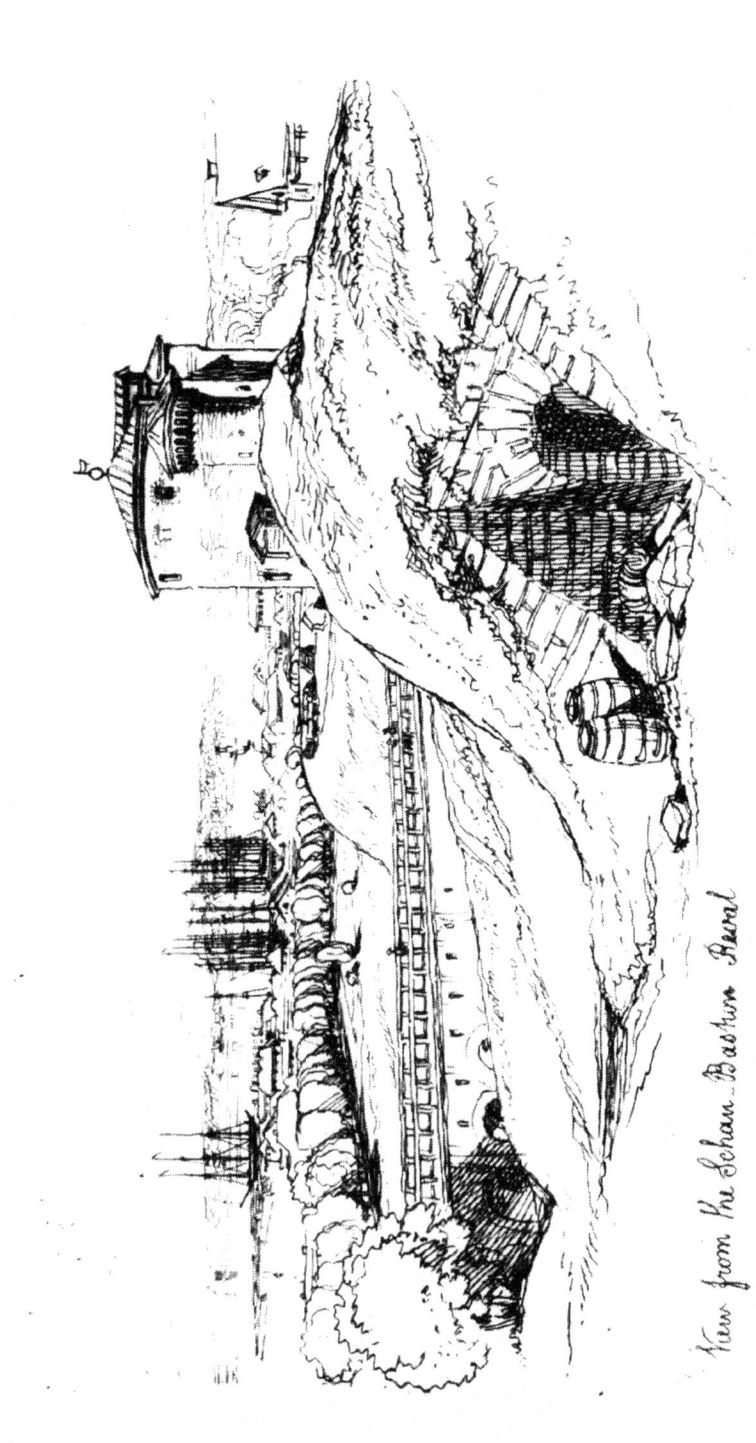

ize their accommodations. Bathing is here conducted very differently from what it is with us:—no chilly early rising with a walk to the beach before the day is aired—no tormentor in the shape of a rough sailor or fat fishwoman to plunge you remorselessly beneath a horrid wave, where you issue blinded, deafened, and stifled, and incomparably colder and crosser than you went in;—but here, when the day is at the hottest, you step leisurely in, like a water-nymph, bathe head and face, nestle gradually beneath the rippling waves, and listen to their soft whispers and dabble with their smooth resistance for twenty minutes if you please; emerging with limbs warm, pliant, and strengthened, and with the most ardent desire for the renewal of this luxury, which may be safely indulged in again the same afternoon. I have seen delicate creatures, who at first were lifted from the carriage to the bathing-house, restored day by day, and in a fortnight's time bathing with a zest that seemed to renew all their energies. Bathing is so indispensable to the Russian, that he makes a study of it, and strengthens himself in summer as thoroughly as he warms himself in winter. Then, when the heat of the day is subsiding, the deep shades of Catherinthal are the universal resort; and equipages and pedestrians line the road from Reval. Here a band of military music plays, and restaurateurs offer ices, chocolate, &c., and you parade about and your friends join you, and you sit down and the gnats sting you; and if you don't like this, you may adjourn to the *salle de danse* close by, where the limbs so late floating listlessly on the waves now twirl round in the hurrying waltz;—and all this is very pleasant for a short time.

The reigning topics in the beau monde, after the Empress's illness and the Grand Duchess's marriage, were the *Lust Fahrte*, or pleasure-trips to Helsingforst—a city which, although merely a six hours' voyage across the gulf, has been only recently discovered by the Estonians. Two years back a few individuals ventured across, and, being entertained with great kindness by the Finlanders, returned with such panegyrical accounts of the charms of Helsingforst, that multitudes followed their example, and the hospitality of the inhabitants has been put to a severe test. These trips, which take place about once a fortnight, have proved a very successful speculation to the projectors, but a particularly sore subject to the shopkeepers of Reval, who, after paying high duty for their goods, are deserted by their customers for the better and cheaper wares of duty-free Finland. Hence it is that the Russian custom-house here out-Russians itself in every vexatious and annoying precaution for counteracting this evil; and, were the explorers of the new region only men, there could be little doubt of their perfect success, but woman's wit has baffled greater tyrants than they. If it be sweet to drive a bargain, how much more so to smuggle it through seeming impossibilities!—Consequently the shopkeepers at home find no greater demand than before these extra regulations were enforced.

Having determined on joining one of these

Lust Fahrte, we soon came in for our share of the tender mercies of the custom-house denizens, who, to make double sure, fall upon you at both ends of your journey. To our bootless indignation, our trunks had to be submitted to their inspection the day before starting, when they took a list of every article they included, extending even to the umbrellas, the same being an item of great attraction at Helsingforst; so that any forgotten article, any innocent pocket-handkerchief or pair of stockings of the most honest descent, not included in the list, ran the risk of condemnation upon our return. This plan had not even the advantage of preparing us betimes for our journey, and when we awoke at five the next morning there were still a thousand things to do, and a thousand to think of—the one remembered without doing, and the other done without thought. So many of the élite of Reval were bound on the same errand, that the whole little town was wide awake at this early hour, and equipages and four thundered down the Domberg without the usual precautions, and jostled each other in the harbour; while no less than a hundred and eighty persons mounted the little steam-boat.

What a mixture of northern nations and dialects were here!—grave Danes and slender Swedes; Russians of every style of physiognomy, European and Asiatic, with strange full names, like water gulping out of a bottle, and a certain air of liveliness and jauntiness, whence the fitting appellation of *le Français du Nord;* and the fat, fubsy, phlegmatic German, the very antithesis of this latter, whose pipe is as a feature of his face, and not always the plainest; all uniting in the one adopted tongue of courtesy, fitness, and pertness—French—and yet not a Frenchman among them all. Many friends and acquaintances were here, and Herrmann B., with the speaking eyes and silent tongue, who saw everything and said nothing; and, by an agreeable accident, it happened that no husband had his wife on board, and no wife her husband, and—'tis true, 'tis pity, pity 'tis 'tis true—these connubial fragments never appeared to better advantage; and, there being nobody to please, all were pleased, and the weather was beautiful, and the sea as even-tempered as the rest. Ourselves were the only unworthy representatives of "that isle which boasts, profuse as vernal blooms, the fairest dames and gentlest swains;" though the many plain Englishwomen and ill-mannered Englishmen who crowd the Continent, it is to be feared, may have shaken a foreigner's faith in this respect.

At first a decent pause was allowed for reserve; then the *avant gardes* of each party exchanged civilities, which thence quickly circulated through the mass, and only a solitary Estonian or two, in whom the spirit of formality seemed embodied, held aloof. The Russians, as the saying goes, "soon feed out of your hand," but they temper the act with a grace which the haughtiest of hearts could not resist. No nation so ingeniously unites the most perfect sluttery with the most perfect good breeding. The same man whose *intacte* manners would fit him for the highest circles will not scruple to exhibit negligences of dress which our lowest would shun—Generals with princely fortunes, affecting a contempt for the effeminacy of whole attire, may be seen at times in threadbare surtouts and boots they might better bestow on their valets; but this *mauvais genre* takes its rise from the highest authority of the Empire, who himself, it is said, occasionally enjoys the relaxation of being out at elbows. Be this as it may, neatness is certainly not an inherent quality in a Russian disposition.

Helsingforst is approached through islands of rocks, some of them only tenanted by fishermen, others massively fortified—especially that called Sweaborg, which is the Cronstadt of this Finnish capital. Nor does the likeness end here, for the town itself, clean and handsomely built, recalls Petersburg upon the first aspect. Tremendous thunder-clouds were gathering over the rocky landscape, and we hurried to the *Societäts Haus,* the only hotel in the town, and a magnificent building, where most of the hundred and eighty found accommodation. Here we were no sooner housed than thunder and lightning burst over the town, but were little heeded in the welcome rattle of knives and forks. The storm subsided into a regular rain, but shopping was not to be neglected—what else did all these good ladies come for?—so we sallied out, buying new umbrellas and Indian-rubber caloshes as we moved along, and laughing at the immediate service these new acquisitions had to perform. And all having much the same errands, and much the same curiosity, we moved from shop to shop, through the streaming and deserted streets, a party of at least thirty, to the great astonishment of the townsfolks. Goods were cheap, but of no great choice; and we could not but admire the military precision of one of these wifeless husbands. Whilst others were debating what first to look at, he came, saw, and chose;—but, unfortunately for his doctrine of promptitude, and more especially for his wife's feelings, they were invariably ugly things.

That evening the theatre advertised a piece in honour of one of our passengers, the lady of a distinguished personage, but we preferred a ball, where we were initiated into the mysteries of a *Suédoise*, a dance with no recommendation but the time it leaves you to improve your partner's acquaintance. The countenances around us were highly uninteresting—light hair and fair complexions plentiful. The belle of the room—and Heaven knows no great beauty was wanting to claim this title—was a Baroness K——, famed for the no very rare gift of portionless beauty, and for her hopeless attachment to an equally empty-handed Russian lieutenant. The Emperor, who, according to this precedent, thought it sweeter to bless one loving pair than "heap rewards on vulgar merit," touched by her faithful love and fading looks, allowed the lady a pension, that she might indulge the one and regain the other. The former has been effected, but the latter probably were too far gone to remedy; and the baroness has retained only that little peculiarity of manner of those ladies who look at their own beauty on the unpoetical side.

The next day, Sunday, was fine. We proposed walking and seeing the granite beauties of the place by sunshine, but Mesdames A., B., and C. intended no such thing. The shops, though shut "*pour préserver les dehors,*" had back doors to them, and those wide open; and one pretty Russian acquaintance argued it to be her duty, as "*une bonne Chrétienne,*" to work out her passage-money in industriously-driven bargains. Here, therefore, we abandoned them, and betook ourselves to the rocks, mounting from one sloping mass to another, till Helsingforst, with its numerous islets, lay beneath us, and from innumerable pits in the rocks glanced pools of clear water from the recent rains; while this Northern Adriatic mirrored a sky full and blue as that of a southern clime. Far as the eye could see, no food for man was visible—no corn-field, grass, or verdure of any kind, except that of the dark pine. Weaving and sail-making are the chief occupations and means of traffic of the Finlanders, and their corn they fetch from our fertile Estonian home. Helsingforst has not a population of more than ten thousand, and bears no remains of any former splendour; its oldest houses being shabby erections of wood, which contrast most disadvantageously with those of stone which have started up since its final cession to Russia at the peace of Friedericksham, in 1809. This part of Finland is included among the Russian *gouvernemens*, and has a governor over it; but justice is administered by a senate of its own, so jealous of authority, that, on occasion of a visit from the present Emperor, who, thinking to conciliate his Finnish subjects, assumed the president's chair in person, the assembly refused to proceed to business, and gave his Majesty to understand that it was against their laws to suffer a stranger to conduct them.

Agreeable to that policy with which Russia treats all newly acquired provinces, they enjoy an exemption from taxes and duties till the year 1850.

Our steps soon led us to the Observatory, a building of recent erection, and vying with that of Dorpat in beauty of apparatus; on the hills opposite to which, and upon about the same level, stands a magnificent church, most appropriately surmounting the town, and, like the Isaac's church in Petersburg, still behung with forests of scaffolding. The university and senate's house are also fine modern buildings; and the Botanic Garden, a little rich plot of ground veneered into the grey rocks, bears witness to the existence of flowers, which otherwise these rock-born natives might have deemed mere fabulous treasures.

Our dinner was a meal of great merriment —above a hundred, including many officers from the garrison, sat down to the sociable table d'hôte, and the little officious waiters slipped and slided round, while another thunder-storm was welcomed as coming at the most opportune hour for all sight-seers. All was now harmony and good cheer; and the guests fisted their knives and forks, and brandished them over their shoulders to the great peril of their neighbours' eyes, and hurled such masses into their mouths as would have given an abstemious Englishman his dinner, when— "lo! what mighty contests spring from trivial things!"—a luckless waiter's foot slipped— down went the main prop of our dinner, and, in the confusion of wiping up which ensued, no one thought to replace the important defaulter. The gentlemen, nearest affected by this loss, first looked angry things, and then said them, and still no joint was forthcoming; when suddenly a pair of soft eyes, which seldom venture above your shoe-tie, sparkled wide open and flashed like the lightning without—a set of teeth, like rows of pearl seen only by greatest favour on occasion of a languid smile, ground themselves from ear to ear—and a voice, hitherto only heard in such accents as a maiden owns her first love, thundered out, "*Bringen Sie das Fleisch gleich, oder ich schmeiss' Sie aus dem Fenster*"— "Bring the meat this moment, or I'll throw you out of the window,"—a menace quite in the Russian Garde officer style. My companion and myself exchanged glances which plainly said, "Can this be the gentle Herrmann?" But Herrmann it certainly was, transformed from the lamb to the lion, whilst his lady-mother, much such another snow-capped volcano as himself, sat by, in no way disconcerted at her son's eruption. The sequel was that the waiter, with German phlegm and true Hamburg grammar, coolly answered, "*Es giebt kein Fleisch mehr, und Sie können mir nicht aus dem Fenster werfen:*"—which must be given in French—"Il n'y a plus de viande, et vous ne pouvez pas *moi* jeter par la fenêtre"—and here the matter ended; but those dove-like eyes deceived us no more.

After dinner, unappalled by an inky sky, we hired, at a rouble each, a little miniature steam-boat, with a machine scarce bigger than a tea-kettle, which whizzed and fumed us about at the will of two Swedish lads, and landed us at Sveaborg. This island is about five acres in extent, loaded with crown buildings and a population of military, and sacred to the memory of Field Marshal Count Ehrensward, whose monument stands here. Thence we steered for the *Scheeren*, literally the Scissars, a beautiful chasm of sea, between meeting and retreating islands, where trees with *leaves* grow by the water's edge; and where the Helsingforstians in their holiday expeditions land and bear off a leaf with as keen a pleasure as we should the choicest bouquet. But " pleasure suits itself to all,—the rich can but be pleased." The rain fell occasionally in torrents around us; but our little puffing bark seemed to bear a charm, or, as a ready Russian officer of the party observed, "*pas un, mais plusieurs;*" and we passed dry on, while some delicious voices on board gave us alternately German and Russian melodies.

There is a luxury in passive enjoyment, with which the smooth motion of the waters seems particularly in unison. Here you ruminate without thought, as you progress without effort; while on the element which wears on its surface no trace of the past, the mind involuntarily wanders back to days gone by for ever, recalling images which early experience or early sorrow—for these are synonymous—has left ineffaceable, and which the easier prudence of a more active hour forbids. Before the voices had ceased, many of our party were living far away in a world of their own, conversing with those to whom no outer object bore reference, while Herrmann, turned again to stone, sat gazing into the waves.

The next morning the first stage of smuggling had commenced; for where were all the accumulated shoppings of Saturday and *Sunday* to be stowed? The trunks, everybody knew, were forbidden ground; so those who went up lean to bed came down plump and comfortable, and those who were stout already stretched a size or two without any inconvenience. One lady stuffed her man-servant, maid-servant, and three children, and still had goods to spare. Another wadded two tall striplings of sons into well-furnished men, who assured us they could lie down on the bare floor on any side with perfect comfort. Old caps and old umbrellas were distributed with the utmost liberality to the waiters, who seemed accustomed to offerings of this kind; and in lieu of these every civilian mounted a light Leghorn hat, and all the world sported new umbrellas. Those who had abstained from the general buying were now in great request; and "Can't you accommodate this small parcel?"—or "Do find a corner just for this shawl,"—or something to that effect—was heard on all sides; and any scruples with regard to defrauding governments, which might be floating in a few individuals, soon melted before the obvious charity of helping your neighbour.

At twelve o'clock we all repaired to the Quay, and mounted the "Fürst Menschikoff," which had arrived the day before from Abo and Stockholm, bringing with it a fresh influx of passengers. Some of our friends also had deserted for a further trip, and, in the exchange, two Englishmen were included, who somewhat tried the feelings of the military Russians on board by mentioning a great *fair* they were about to visit at Moscow, which on further inquiry turned out to be a review of all the Imperial troops. The sea this time did not treat us so well as before. One half of the passengers were ill, and the other half by no means well. But a cold east wind blew us over, and in less than six hours' time the dim outline of the Domberg at Reval was visible.

Ere long the custom-house harpies were upon us, and, knowing how singularly the air of Helsingforst had fattened our party, I must own I trembled with apprehension. But the first few passed muster with a courage worthy of a better cause, and which inspired their followers with confidence. Various scrutinising taps and pats were received with perfect sang froid, or repelled with dignified innocence; and I believe the whole party came off safe,—doubtless to boast of their smuggling deeds for the rest of their lives. For here to outwit a custom-house officer is as much a feather in cap as the Irishman's deceit of the exciseman.

LETTER THE EIGHTEENTH.

Reval at Midsummer — Antiquities — Gates — Churches — Dance of Death — The Duke de Croy — Hôtel de Ville — Corps of the Schwarzen Häupter — Towers — Antiquities of the Domberg — Kotzebue — The Jahr Markt, and its varied population — Catherinthal — The water-party — Visit to a Russian man-of-war.

At this sultry season our residence upon the Domberg is particularly agreeable. Here every sea-breeze from the glistening and rippled bay sweeps in grateful coolness over us, and leaf and streamer on our rocky eminence are seen fluttering in the freshened air, while the heated streets lie in burning stillness below. During the day's meridian no one, uncompelled, stirs from home, but towards evening, if such it may be called where we retire to rest by broad daylight at eleven at night, we call together a few choice spirits, and loiter from one *hof* or court to another, drinking in all the beauties of Gothic tower, ruined convent, misty island, and orient cloud, waiting for the evening gun from the Russian men-of-war in the harbour, or for the gay clarion from the Russian churches; when, careless of time and spendthrift of light, we gradually descend the embankment, crossing over archways and under tunnels, and running down green slopes, till we find ourselves at one of the town gates, and with shortened breaths are constrained to climb to our eagle's eyrie on the Dome again. And a couple of lovers are in our train—harmless beings, whose transient happiness we favour, and who invariably fall behind and follow us like sleep-walkers—knowing no fatigue;—till the very sentinels respect their reveries, and silently motion them the path we have taken. And when, weary with the long walk and ceaseless light, we are separating for the night, they artlessly ask, "*Wollen sie nicht weiter gehen?*"—won't you walk farther?— and, like children, never know when they have enough.

Old house Reval

But now you must descend with us into the narrow streets of the town, which we explore with the freedom of foreigners and intimacy of natives, but where we take no lovers to fetter our footsteps. Whoever has seen Hamburg and Lübeck, or the Netherlandish towns, will recognise that Reval has participated in the same Hanseatic bond. The irregular, many-storied houses — their gables towards the street—with the ample garret above and the spacious hall beneath, betokening room equally for the rich merchant's goods and the rich merchant's hospitality — the Gothic-arched doorways, approached by flights of steps, with projecting spaces on each side, with stone benches where families in olden times sate before their doors in sociable converse, many of which are now removed by order of the Emperor, as contracting too much the width of the streets—the old Hôtel de Ville—the many ancient churches, towers, and gateways—all these features perpetually remind the traveller of its many sister cities of similar ancient importance and present decay, and present an aspect which one of the young Grand Duchesses has in court language pronounced to be "*parfaitement rococo.*"

Like ancient Thebes, Reval is entered by seven gates, viz. the great Strandpforte, the lesser Strandpforte, the Lehmpforte, the Karripforte, the Schmiedepforte, the Sisternpforte, and the Dompforte. These are all picturesque erections, decorated with various historical mementos—the arms of the Danish domination, or the simple cross of the Order, or the municipal shield of the city, &c. The Schmiedepforte is noted as being the scene of an act of daring magisterial justice, which took place in 1535. At all times a petty animosity had existed between the rich burghers of Reval and the lawless nobility of the province, who troubled the commerce and derided the laws of the former, and were by no means induced to a pacific mode of life by the example of their knights. At the time alluded to, however, the atrocious murder of one of his own peasants in the streets of Reval by Baron Üxküll of Riesenberg, one of the most powerful nobles of the country, so greatly excited the ire of the city magistracy, that they menaced the offender, should he ever be found within their jurisdiction, with the utmost severity of the law. Nevertheless, despising their threat and with the insolence of one who acknowledged no law, Baron Üxküll entered the city in mere bravado, attended by a slender retinue—was seized, condemned, and, in full view of his friends without the walls, executed beneath the Schmiedepforte. Long and sanguinary were the disputes that followed upon this act, and, as some pacification to Üxküll's memory, the burghers walled up the gateway, which was not re-opened till the beginning of this century.

The churches of Reval are numerous, comprising Lutheran, Greek, Swedish, and Roman Catholic places of worship. The Lutheran are of the greatest antiquity. To speak of the church of Saint Olai under this head may seem paradoxical, since the edifice of this name, which was originally built in 1329, and has been struck and partially consumed by lightning no less than eight times, is now only just risen from the ashes in which it was finally laid in 1820. Its archives and library, however, preserve an unbroken history; and many of its architectural ornaments, coeval with its earliest erection, have been saved from the flames. Among the former is a piece of sculpture of great richness, consisting of two wide niches, the upper one empty, the lower occupied by a skeleton with a toad resting on the body and a serpent crawling out of the ear—supposed to typify the destruction of an idol image, recorded to have been filled with these reptiles; —and with a gorgeous breadth of stone-work in eight partitions around, exhibiting the triumph of Christianity in the passion of our Saviour, and other parts of the New Testament. This bears date 1513. The tower of St. Olai, which has been rebuilt precisely on the former scale and form, is about 250 English feet high, and serves as a landmark in navigation. This edifice, the cathedral church of the lower town, is in pure early Gothic, with lancet windows of great beauty, and dedicated to St. Olai, a canonized king of Norway, who mounted the throne at the beginning of the eleventh century, and first introduced Christianity among the Norwegians.

The next church in importance is that of St. Nicholas—a large, three-aisled structure with massive square tower—built by Bishop Nicholas in 1317. This appears to have eluded the zeal of the iconoclasts of reforming times, who throughout Estonia seem to have been as hasty in stripping the churches as her doctors were in denuding the creed, and possesses many relics of Roman Catholic times. The most interesting are the pictures of the altar, especially two wing paintings containing small half-length figures of bishops, cardinals, priests, and nuns—three on each side—in Holbein's time and manner, on a blue ground, and of great beauty. Also a picture, placed for better lighting at the back of the altar—a Crucifixion, including the two thieves, with town and mountains in the background, and a procession of equestrian figures entering the gate. This is of singular beauty of expression and form, though much injured by recent renovations—of the school of Raphael, and especially in the manner of Andrea del Salerno.

Immediately at the entrance of the church on the right hand is a representation of the oft-repeated Dance of Death—coinciding not only in age and arrangement, but also word for word in the Platt Deutsch verses beneath, with the same subject in St. Mary's church at Lübeck—in some instances each mutually assisting the other's deficiency. The beginning, including the Pope, the Emperor, the Empress, the Cardinal, and the King, which, if I mistake not, are failing in Lübeck, are here preserved. The rest is lost or defaced, though the inscriptions are in a few cases still legible—and terminating with "*Dat Wegenkind to dem Dode*" the cradle-child to Death,—with this naïve couplet:

"O Dot! wo shal ik dat vorstan!
Ik shal danssen, un kan nicht ghan!"

or, in good German,

"O Tod! wie soll ich dass verstehen!
Ich soll tanzen, und kann nicht gehen!"—

which we may thus render in English :—

> Oh Death! what's the use of all this talk!
> Would you have me dance before I can walk?

But the peculiar drollery of Platt Deutsch is unattainable in a more cultivated tongue.

The chapels of some of the chief nobility, with massive iron gates and richly adorned with armorial bearings, are attached to this church, though all in a very neglected state. The Rosen chapel is now occupied by the unburied body of a prince, who expiates in this form a life of extravagance. The Duke de Croy—a Prince of the Roman Empire, Markgraf of Mount Cornette, and of other fiefs, &c., and descended from the kings of Hungary—after serving with distinction under the Emperor of Austria and King of Poland, passed over to the service of Peter the Great, obtained the command of the Russian army, and was defeated by Charles XII. at the battle of Narva. Fearing the Zar's resentment, he surrendered to the enemy, and was sent a prisoner at large to Reval, which has been, and is still, the scene of honourable banishment for state prisoners, and which at that epoch was yet under the sway of Sweden. Here, indulging a passion for ostentation, he managed to spend so much, that though only a few years elapsed between his removal to Reval and his death, the residue of his fortune was unequal to meet his debts, upon which the numerous creditors, availing themselves of an old law, which refuses the rites of sepulture to insolvent debtors, combined to deny him a Christian burial, and the body was placed in a cellar in the precincts of this church. It might be imagined that, when these said relentless creditors were not only dead, but, unlike their noble debtor, buried also, the Duke de Croy would have found a resting-place; but when that time came, all who had profited, as well as all those who had lost by his extravagance were gone also, and their descendants cared little how he had lived or how he had died. So the body remained in its unconsecrated abode, until, accident having discovered it, in 1819, in a state of perfect preservation owing to the anti-putrescent properties of the cold, it was removed into the

Rosen chapel, and now ranks among the lions of this little capital. The corpse is attired in a rich suit of black velvet and white satin, equally uninjured by the tooth of time—with silk stockings, full curled wig, and a ruff of the most exquisite point lace, which any modern Grand Duchess might also approve. The remains are those of a small man, with an aristocratic line of countenance. There is something at all times imposing in viewing the cast-off dwelling of an immortal spirit— that clay which weighs down our better portion, and which, though so worthless in itself, is so inexpressibly dear to those who love us, and so tenaciously clung to by ourselves. Life had quitted this tenement 138 years. The old Sacristan, a little shrivelled mummy of a man, scarcely more human-looking than the body before us, profits in his creature comforts by the exhibition of this dust, which he stroked and caressed with something of gratitude and fellow-feeling, and, locking the ponderous door, ejaculated, " *Da liegt mein bester Freund!* "—

"There lies my best friend!" Poor Duke de Croy!

In respect of antiquity the Estonian church bears off the palm in Reval—being mentioned by Jean Bishop of Reval, when he granted to the city the " *Jus ecclesiasticum et episcopale*," after the form of the Lübeck statute, in 1284— a time when St. Olai and St. Nicholas did not exist.

The Russian church, or one adapted to the Russian service in later times, is also of great antiquity, but has been altered to the external type of all Greek places of worship.

The Hôtel de Ville has been also renovated with windows of modern form, which possess no recommendation beyond that of admitting more light. Within, the magisterial chair is still held in the empty and worn-out forms of days of more importance, and the effigy of the burgher who had his tongue cut out for divulging a state secret, warns his successors of less responsible times to be more discreet.

Several Guildhalls, with groined roofs, tell

of those corporations of merchants who here met for business or feasting, and are now passed away with the commerce of Reval: with the exception, however, of the corps of the *Schwarzen Häupter, les Frères têtes-noires*—so called probably from their patron saint, St. Mauritius—a military club of young merchants formed in 1343, for the defence of the city. These were highly considered—were endowed by the Masters of the Order with the rank and privileges of a military body—wore a peculiar uniform—had particular inauguration ceremonies and usages—and bore their banner, " *aut vincendum aut moriendum,*" on many occasions most gallantly against the numberless foes who coveted the riches of Reval. Every young apprentice was required, on pain of a heavy fine, to enter this corps upon the first year of his domiciliation in Reval, and each new brother was welcomed with solemn observances, and plentiful draughts of beer, now substituted by wine.

On some occasions this corps suffered severely, and a defaced monument on the Pernau road, a few wersts from the walls of Reval, attests the slaughter of many of their numbers by the Russians in 1500. Each successive sceptre has acknowledged their rights—Peter the Great became a member, and himself inscribed his name in their registers. Catherine II. granted their chief the rank of a captain in the Russian army. Alexander was admitted to the brotherhood, and ordained that the banner should thenceforth receive the military salute; and Nicholas, equally recognising the ancient deeds or present harmlessness of the Order, has deviated from his general condemnation of all associations, and is himself an Imperial Schwarzhäupt. The last time that this corps was summoned for the defence of the city was on occasion of the Swedish invasion in 1790. The chief edifice where they held their meetings is curiously adorned in front with the Moor's head and other armorial pieces of sculpture; but within it has been stripped of all antiquity, excepting the archives of the Order, and portraits of the various crowned heads and Masters of the Livonian Order who

Der lange Herrmann

have held Estonia in their sway. The altarpiece from the convent of St. Brigitta—a magnificent ruin upon the sea-coast in full view of Reval—is also placed here, being a piece in three compartments, in the Van Eyck manner, comprising God the Father, with the Infant Saviour in the centre—the Virgin on the one hand, the Baptist on the other—and greatly recalling portions of the famous altar-piece painted for St. Bavon's church at Ghent. On the back of the two wings, and closing over the centrepiece, is the subject of the Annunciation—two graceful figures in grey, of later Italian date.

This is but an inadequate sketch of the antiquities of this city, which is further strewn with the ruined remains of convents and monasteries of considerable interest, though too much choked with parasitical buildings to be seen to any advantage. The outer circumference is bound in with walls and towers of every irregular form, most of which have significant names, as for instance, "*der lange Herrmann,*" a singularly beautiful and lofty circular tower crowning the dome; and "*die dicke Marguerite"*—a corpulent erection lower in the town.

The dome is equally stored with traces of olden times—consisting of the old castle, which encloses an immense quadrangle, and is in part appropriated to the governor's residence;—the Dome Church, a building of incongruous architecture, filled with tombs of great interest, of the Counts De la Gardie, Thurn, Horn, &c., beneath which lie the vaults of several corporations of trade, variously indicated—the shoemakers' company by the bas relief of a colossal boot in the pavement—the butchers' by an ox's head, &c. Further on is the Ritterschaft's Haus, or Hôtel de la Noblesse, where the Landräthe assemble, the Landtag is held, and all the business connected with the aristocracy of the province conducted. Every family of matriculated nobility has here its shield of arms and date of patent; while on tablets of white marble are inscribed the names of all the noble Estonians who served in the French campaign, and on tables of black marble the names of those who fell;—and truly

Estonia has not been niggardly of her best blood. The archives of the Ritterschaft do not date beyond 1590, all preceding documents having perished on a voyage to Sweden; but important additions have been made by the researches of the well-known German writer Kotzebue, among the secret state papers of the Teutonic Order at Königsberg.

Kotzebue spent several years at Reval, actively engaged in disseminating those doctrines of so-called freedom and equality which followed in the train of the French revolution, and were further promulgated by the publication of Göthe's Wahlverwandschaften. And much private misery, the traces of which still remain, ensued to this province by the adoption of chimerical schemes of happiness, which consisted in little more than in yielding to each new inclination in turn, and throwing off all old ties as they lost their attraction. Nor, it is just to add, did Kotzebue himself hesitate to practise what he too successfully preached. First one Estonian lady pleased him, and became his wife; but a year or two after, another pleased him still better, and the first was divorced; and, strange to say, before this votary of the law of reason was suited to his mind, a third, best of all, appeared. His murder at Manheim, by Sandt the student, was the sequel to his residence in Russia; and more than one of his widows, I believe, and several of his descendants, still remain in Estonia.

The *Jahrmarkt*, or annual fair, is now going forward in Reval. This is held in a most picturesque spot, beneath the old elm trees before the church of St. Nicholas; the low wide-roofed booths surmounted with their different insignia, with wares of all colours floating around them, and merchants of all complexions swarming before them, while the venerable trees and time-worn edifice look down in sober grandeur on all this short-lived bloom. In old times, every merchant of any consideration in Reval removed to his booth in the fair, and old customers were welcomed to old goods; and though the one was not less dear, nor the other less difficult, yet both buyer and seller equally enjoyed the gaiety of the time, and were satisfied with this social gain. But now Reval mankind is becoming soberer, and by tacit consent it has been agreed that as no superiority in the goods, nor accession in the demand, accompanies this change of place, it is as well to leave the merchandise in its place on the counter, instead of flaunting it forth beneath the old trees in the churchyard. The Jahrmarkt is therefore gradually being abandoned to the travelling merchants from countries widely severed, who peregrinate from one mart to another, and, save the same sovereign, own no social element or bond in common. Here were Russians with their Siberian furs, and Bulgarians with their Turkish clothes, and Tula merchants with their cutlery—all infinitely more interesting to the foreigner than the wares they displayed. And before his booth lolled the sleepy Tartar, with flat face, and high cheek-bones, and little eyes which opened and shut on his customers with a languor and expression often absent from orbs of twice the dimensions—and beside him paced the grave Armenian, with long nose and high peaked forehead and searching glance—neither comprehending the other, and both accosting me in Russian scarce superior to mine own. "The *Sudarina* is no *Nyemka*," "The Signora is no German," said the shrewd Armenian—*Nyemki,* or the dumb, being the appellation given to the first German settlers, whose ignorance of Russian reduced them to a compulsory silence, and since bestowed on the whole nation—"Whence does the *Sudarina* come?" "*Ya Anglichanka,*" "I am an Englishwoman," I replied; an avowal abroad, like that of a patrician name at home, never otherwise than agreeable to make, and, thinking to increase his respect, added, "and my home is two thousand wersts off." "*Eto nichavo,*" "that's nothing," said the Armenian, with a smile not unmixed with disdain, "my wife and children live six thousand wersts hence." Nor is this by any means an extreme case—the Petersburg post penetrates to inland homes fourteen thousand wersts removed from the monarch's residence.

This Jahrmarkt is the morning lounge—

Catherinthal the evening promenade. It may be as well to mention here, that this latter resort is an imperial *Lustschloss,* or summer palace, surrounded with fine trees and well-kept grounds, or what is here termed "*ein superber Park,*" which every evening during six weeks in the summer are thronged with fashionable groups like our Zoological Gardens on a Sunday. This residence, which is literally a bower of verdure redeemed from a waste of sand, is the pleasant legacy of Peter the Great to the city of Reval. Being a frequent visitor to Reval, it was here that he first erected a modest little house beneath the rocks of the Laaksberg, from the windows of which he could overlook his infant fleet riding at anchor in the bay, and which still exists. But a few years previous to his death, the present palace within a stone's throw of his Dutch house,—for all Peter the Great's own private domiciles testify whence he drew his first ideas of comfort,—was constructed, which he surrounded with pleasure-grounds, and presented to his consort by the name of Catherinthal. This gift he increased by the purchase of surrounding estates to the value of several millions of roubles*—sufficient to have assured to the empress, in case of need, a fitting retreat from the frowns of Russian fortune. These estates have been gradually alienated and bestowed on private individuals, and Catherinthal is reduced to little more than its gardens. It has been the temporary sojourn of all the crowned heads of Russia in succession; and the treaty of peace concerning Silesia, between the two most powerful women of coeval times whom the world has ever known—Maria Theresa of Austria and Catherine II. of Russia—was here ratified in 1746.

Nevertheless, whoever prefers the sweet influences of Nature, uninterrupted by silks and satins, and uniforms and noisy music, must visit Catherinthal in the early morning, when

* The Russian rouble, like the German florin, is a piece of money only current in the imagination, there being no coin of this value in actual circulation. It tallies with the franc in amount, and is worth ten pence, though at this time the rate of exchange is much against the traveller, and every rouble costs him eleven pence and upwards. The silver rouble is a distinct coin, and is worth three roubles and a half.

a sweeter spot for the enjoyment of solitude, or of that better happiness, a congenial mind, heart, and taste, cannot be desired. It seems that beneath this dry surface of sand the trees have found a rich soil, for vegetation is here of the utmost southern luxuriance, and the thick mat of foliage around and above only reveals occasional glimpses of the grey rocks or line of blue sea beyond. Or, if you wish to break from this thicket, you have only to climb a rugged path up the rocks, whence all this verdure is seen wreathed in rich festoons at your feet, and above this luxuriant green carpet lies Reval with its spires and towers in stripes of varying light and shade—the proud Domberg rising like a gigantic citadel, or Gothic Acropolis, in the midst: while half surrounding the city spreads the cool placid sea, and little tongues of land carry the abodes of man far into the waters, and deep bays carry the waters high into the shores; and the eye quits towers and domes for masts and shrouds, and further still rests on a solitary fortress insulated in the sea—the last bond between the crowded city and the huge men-of-war lying beyond. And behind all are the misty islands of the Baltic; and above all a midsummer morning sky, hazy with growing heat, and speckled with a few lazy clouds.

But after having gazed your fill—after having drank deep of the beauties of earth and sky—how sweeter far it is to turn to a countenance whose features never pall, and whose loveliness knows no winter—to eyes, by turns soft with emotion, or brilliant with intellect, where the deepest shade of sorrow is ever cheered by a gleam of playfulness, and the brightest mood of merriment chastened by a shade of sentiment; and which now turn, as if spell-bound, to claim and render back those speechless looks of affection for which Nature's richest array has no equivalent! Such moments are the diamonds in the dark mine of memory—such looks, the stars which forsake us not when life's other suns are set.

After such a morning as this, who would wish to see this hallowed ground desecrated by training gowns and jingling spurs? No!—

Earth has nothing better to offer; and now the sea becomes the element of our desire. A few courteous words therefore to some *Flott-officier* of our acquaintance place a Russian brig-boat at our disposal, and descending the harbour-pier we launch into the deep, bearing with us some of those bright eyes and witty tongues which I have feebly described as the *points d'appui* in Reval society; and ere we have quitted the land's warm atmosphere, both are in such active play, that the young lieutenant who has the command of the boat, and the elderly general who has the charge of the party, both equally forget their vocation. But nothing is said that might not be uttered anywhere, or would not be enjoyed everywhere; while in the peals of laughter which ring along the silent waters, one voice, in which the very soul of mirth seems articulated, vibrates above every other, and the rocks of the Laaksberg, or the lofty façade of St. Brigitta's convent, rising boldly from the waves, send back the merry echoes, and there is not a stroller on the shore but may recognise beyond all doubt that

Baron C. is of this aquatic party. Even the sailors catch the infection, and brush their coarse sleeves across their faces as much to conceal their laughter as to wipe away the streaming perspiration. Otherwise there was little pleasurable to them in this expedition. Several of the rowers were Estonians lately drafted into the navy, and as yet unable to comprehend the loud Russian vociferations of a tyrannical boatswain, as often prefaced as seconded by blows. Poor men! the spectacle of their hard lives checked many a bright laugh.

Before returning to our homes we visited one of the Russian men-of-war which lay without the harbour, and ascending the ship's side were politely received by the officer on guard. Unfortunately I know too little of the interior of an English ship of corresponding rank to offer any comparisons; nor would those of a woman at best be greatly desirable. To all appearance there was cleanliness and comfort; and the sailors, or sea-soldiers as they might be better termed, for they differ but little from those on land save in the colour of their clothes, were loitering and talking together in cheerful groups between decks.

But now the roll of the drum was heard, and numbers hastened to the evening drill on deck —a necessary portion of a sailor's routine on a sea hardly navigable six months in the year—at the conclusion of which, the drummer, a wild-looking little Circassian, in a piebald uniform which assorted well with his dark tints and flashing eyes, commanded attention with a lengthened roll, and then in nearly as monotonous a sound repeated the Lord's Prayer in Russian, as fast as his tongue would permit—this being a part of the service—and with this the body broke up. Among the groups our well-practised eyes sought and found many an Estonian physiognomy, and passing the sentinel at the gangway, who bore the very shepherd on his countenance, one of our arch companions whispered " *Yummal aga.*" A ray of pleasure shot over the poor man's face, though his body remained immoveable as the beam at his side.

LETTER THE NINETEENTH.

Excessive heat—Gnats and gnat-bites—Sleepless nights—Ruins of Padis Kloster—Landrath R.—Baltisport—Leetz—The Island of Little Rogö—Unexpected encounter—Russian builders—A day in the woods—Family parties—Mode of salutation—Old-fashioned manners—Conversation—English pride and German pride—Jealousy of Russian tendencies—Marriages between Russians and Estonians.

THE summer is come, and the summer is going.—Our longest day has blazed itself out, and an unconscionably long day it was, though I knew as little of its ending as of its beginning. Every creature is busy in the hayfield, including all the men-servants, and even some supernumerary maids, who think this change of work as good as play;—I proposed the same to my Sascha, but was checked by a mute look of dignity—and all reminds us to make haste, and bustle about our own haycocks of various denominations, before this fleet-winged season be gone for ever. But as fast as the fine weather urges, the intolerable heat forbids exertion; and here, while every thought of the community centres in ingenious devices for protection from cold, no one dreams of taking precautions against the heat. Thus the summer, like a rare visitor, is made much of—welcomed with open arms, caressed and flattered, and even so little as a thin blind grudged between you and the sudden ardour of its friendship;—while winter, the good old constant family friend, who silently prepares the harvest which summer only reaps, is slandered in its absence, snubbed in its presence, and has doors and windows slammed in its face by high and low without ceremony. What is worse, no one here has any sympathy for a foreigner whose clay was never intended to stand this baking. If I say I am hot, they tell me I ought to be happy;—if I complain I can't sleep, I'm answered, it's a shame to lie in bed while the sun is high in the heavens;—and if I show my burning gnat-bites, a fit of laughter ensues, or, among the better behaved, a compliment on my English *süsses Blut*, or sweet blood, which seems thus in request. I would compound with the incessant light and heat if it were not for these tormenting accompaniments. But capricious summer says, love me, love my gnats, and no one thinks of lifting a hand against these sacred emblems. In Sascha, however, I find one sympathizing heart—she won't make hay with her pretty dimpled hands, but she won't let the gnats bite them either. Therefore as soon as the vapours of evening begin to arise, I hear my windows' fastening sound, and then, slap, slap goes the pretty hand, and the first word that greets me on entering my room for the night, is "*Komar nietto*," no gnats. To bed therefore I go with the happy consciousness of possessing a servant who can equally mend my gloves, correct my speech, and kill my gnats, and, if possible, infuse a kinder tone than usual into my *prostchai*, or farewell for the night.

Scarcely, however, have her retiring footsteps died in the distance, than whiz, whiz— goes something in my ear; and after the first bustle of defence has subsided, there I spy the miscreant standing on his long legs just beyond my reach. "Well, Sascha must have overlooked one!" so, him despatched, I sink down again more secure than ever. And soon my senses fall into a delicious kind of nether state, and then one by one begin to steal away; that of hearing being the last to desert its post. And now, strange to say, I am walking upon the dusty high road, carrying the very bundle of linen under my arm which Sascha was working upon the day before, and stop at an old castle with magnificent high walls, and a row of arched cloisters adjoining, and all close to our own dwelling, though I never observed them before. But all the architectural ornaments alter strangely as I approach them—some look like horses' heads, and others like pewter basins, and it becomes so dark I can hardly grope about, and though I entered the castle conveniently enough by a wide door, I can hardly squeeze myself through the same on returning. And all this time my bundle is greatly in my way, and still I get no nearer home; when suddenly before me stands Sammucka the Russian coachman, with a strange kind of round hat upon his head, turning a grindstone—whirl, whirl,—what a noise that grindstone makes! and pieces fly off red hot and fall among my hair, and on to my cheek, and I stand rooted to the spot without the power to stir. And then the noise subsides, and then increases again louder than ever, whirl, whirl,—whiz, whiz,—and, starting up, Sammucka, grindstone, castle, bundle, all disappear, and in their place remains a fresh gnat-bite, burning like a volcano in the very centre of my cheek. Thus the night passes, and when towards morning I am hoping to retrieve some of my miseries, pat comes a fly with its cold wet proboscis on my forehead, and another on my chin, and as fast as I chase them away they return, and half a dozen quarrel on my very nose. In short, I rise no more refreshed than

I laid down, and I am always put off with praises of their summer, and warnings of its temporary duration; though were it only ten days long, I tell them I must sleep.

These are a most venomous kind of gnat, and might more rightly be termed musquitoes; and, what is worse, you never know when the fire of these little craters is to subside—an accidental rub will set one of a month old burning beyond all endurance. The farther north you go, the more do they swarm. In the short blistering reign of a Siberian summer, no one can go without a mask, and the Laplanders live in smoke to be rid of them. Heaven defend me from such summers; their winters I never complained of.

But to return to subjects of more interest— we have resumed our researches after the ancient and the picturesque. Accident had brought to our knowledge the existence of the ruins of *Padis Kloster*, a name of frequent recurrence in Estonian history, and as it cost only a drive of nineteen wersts to ascertain that which no other taste could determine, the Speise Korb was packed up, and ourselves soon seated beneath the shade of as fine a ruin as Estonia can offer; with every adjunct of old moat, and contemporary tree, and that air of grandeur which clings to a spot after its worldly importance and less picturesque repair have declined. This monastery is mentioned as such in the beginning of the fourteenth century, when, owing to starvation without its walls, and doubtless a very comfortable life within, the peasants rose in numbers around, murdered the abbot and twenty-eight of the monks, and otherwise so devastated the place, that, in 1448, it received a further and full consecration at the hands of Heinrich, Baron Üxküll, Bishop of Reval, at which time it was ordained that whoever should in any way enrich or benefit this *Kloster* of Padis, should, for any sins he might commit, have forty days of penance struck off. Hence perhaps arose the peculiar repute and custom in the sale of indulgences which this monastery enjoyed. Now, however, it stands utterly forgotten, and the stranger within its gates was infinitely a greater object of interest to the passers by than all the mute lessons, moral, historical, or picturesque, of its grey stones.

One mode of rescuing it from oblivion, of fair promise, however, lies in the circumstance of its present proprietor, Landrath R., having been blessed within sight of its ruins with a family of three and twenty children; who, born in a house infinitely too confined to be conveniently the theatre of this domestic fecundity, have successively stretched their six and forty little legs in innocent sports within its walls, to the unspeakable relief of their Frau Mamma, and to their own great physical advantage. The name of Padis Kloster may therefore safely calculate on being bequeathed in grateful odour to a wide-spreading generation, which, mayhap, may prove a shorter process than that of awakening a taste for historical antiquity among the Estonian nobility; who, though sufficiently removed in period, are still too nearly allied to various feudal manners and customs to attach to them any poetic sentiment. Some call it the wilful blindness of the human mind ever to prefer by-gone times to the present, but it may rather be termed a most exquisite provision of Nature which leads us to respect the past like the memory of the dead, and retain of it only what is beautiful and good.

From Padis Kloster, a short journey brought us on to Baltisport, a small seaport never before acknowledged in the range of my geography, about fifty wersts south of Reval, where vessels land their cargoes before the ice admits them higher, and whence thousands of orange and lemon casks are transported by land on to St. Petersburg. The whole range of coast in this direction consists of an elevated table-land descending with magnificent precipitous cliffs into the sea. In some parts these cliffs are four hundred feet in height, shelving inwards, while the waves roar at their bases, and chafe round huge angular masses of rock which have detached themselves from above. In others, the sea retreating has left a little moist strip of rich land, bound in between the

Baltsport.

cliffs and its shores, where vegetation of a southern luxuriance is found, and where the black alder, the only fit substitute for the oak, appears in unrivalled splendour. This sheltered breadth forms part of an estate called Leetz, in the possession of M. de Ramm, whose house, a small wooden building, with a peculiarly peaked roof, "high up to the top," as a Russian surveyor with loyal accuracy once reported of a crown chimney, evinces both the taste and moral courage of his predecessors, for it is built on a rising slope in full view of the sea and of every other beauty.

Upon the highest ground, near Baltisport, stands a lighthouse of great importance in navigation, which here, owing to the many islands crowding the coast, is of considerable difficulty. This circumstance is supposed to have deterred Peter the Great from placing his capital on this part of the coast. Catherine II., however, thought much of Baltisport, and projected a harbour of unrivalled depth and magnitude, by uniting the coast by a gigantic mole to the island of Rogö, three wersts off. But something intervened to stop the work, and nothing is now visible but a restless line of water, where whole mountains of stones have been sunk, and a beautiful mass of masonry butting from the cliff, which the winds and weather have tempered to much the same tints. Baltisport is a wretched little fishing town, with only a Russian church for its mingled population,—though a pious Baron is about to erect a Lutheran one,—and in summer is visited by a few of the neighbouring families for its excellent bathing.

It was bombarded by the English in 1803, who, by the time they had unroofed one house, which still remains a monument of injured innocence, discovered that the inhabitants would be rather glad to welcome them than not. Accordingly they landed, and became very good friends with the little community, who, to do them justice, have never forgotten that their invaders observed that humanity which few of their own allies would have done, viz., paid handsomely for all they took.

Baltisport is famous for its *strömlings*, with which the atmosphere seems impregnated; and has further distinguished itself by a petition to government, of rather a rare nature, *i. e.* to be allowed to *sink into obscurity*—the rights of a township, which Catherine II. bestowed on it, being too expensive an honour to keep up.

As the weather continued fine, and the time spent in viewing general scenery hangs heavy on hand, an excursion was proposed to the neighbouring island, three wersts off, which had thus narrowly escaped a junction with the main land. After rowing half an hour we landed on a flat stony shore, and, leaving our boat, wandered into the country. This islet, called the Little Rogö, is about six wersts in circumference, and lies opposite the Great Rogö, about three times the size; both of which, in former times, belonged to Padis Kloster, and as early as 1345 were pledged to four noblemen for the sum of thirty marks of silver. On this little platform are two villages with well-cultivated corn-fields, and boulder-stones of such enormous size, that we mistook them for ruined towers in the distance. But nothing remains of the forests which, from the reservation of "timber for building," among other rights retained by the monastery, are implied to have existed. It so happened that M. de Ramm, to whom this islet now belongs, had been collecting his dues this very day. At the first village, therefore, we came in for the results of a feast—in other words, all the Little Rogö world was very drunk. Strange to say, this half-hour's transition had ushered us into another language, for Swedish is spoken here, with a little Estonian. Our party was not able to profit by either, for Russian and Lettish were all the northern tongues that could be mustered between us. Our communication was therefore restrained to looks, good-tempered as theirs, and I trust a little more intelligent. Returning to the beach and indulging in a little English to my dear companion, after doing duty in German all the day, we observed a venerable old fisherman eyeing us with great attention, and, setting foot into the boat, to our great astonishment he tottered up to us, and, laying one brown hand on my arm, emphatically said, "God bless you, tell me, are you really English?" His amazement could hardly surpass our own at hearing English tones in this remote spot. He had left his tiny native land to see the world, and served in the English merchant-service thirty-two years. His wife had followed him, and resided at Deptford during his peregrinations. And now the old couple were returned to their wild island to end their days. Strange transition! but the love of home, begun in childhood, flies off during the busy prime of life, and returns to bear old age company. The old man had still English habits about him—he was neat, and clean-shaven, and, pointing to his fishing habiliments, said, "Ah! I am dirty now, but I have clean clothes at my cottage, and an English Bible, and other books." He helped to shove us off, and then stood looking after us, and that distant island now claimed an affinity with us which we had never anticipated.

Returning home, the heat of the weather

again brought lassitude on man and beast, and our days were only varied by a walk, fore and after noon, to the recreating waters of a neighbouring stream; pausing on our way to talk with the groups of Russians who lay reclining after their work beneath the shade of a half-erected building.* The Russian is a builder by nature; the little hatchet in his hand is the emblem of his life. No buildings are here undertaken by Estonian workmen, but these Russians wander the country in quest of work, and are engaged from one estate to another. They were greatly interested in hearing something of that remote island *Anglia,* and only wondered how we could build there without Russians! Courtesy pervades every class; the Russian serf takes off his *fouraschka* with the dignity of a prince, and waits on a lady with the devotion of a slave. Though the tones of the lower orders may be broader, yet they are native grammarians, and speak the language with per-

* However hot the summer of Estonia, it is almost invariably accompanied by a brisk wind—so much so, that Kotzebue remarked that instead of *Esthland,* it were better termed *Windland.*

fect purity. Hence I generally profited by these humble teachers, and returned home with new words to spite Sascha. Then towards eight o'clock the droschky appears at the door, and we drive where we list—into the meadows, which are like vast flower-beds of the gayest colours,—for nowhere have I seen a wild botany of such beauty as here, where flowers which we rear in gardens, the blue campanula, and the justly-named Siberian larkspur, bloom in native luxuriance;—and peasant children meet us with curious baskets made of birch-bark, filled with wild strawberries and raspberries, better than any cultivated fruit I have here tasted, and ten kopecks* buy fruit, basket, and all;—or we take a natural *chaussée* into the woods, and there alighting wander about under vast trunks of Scotch and spruce fir, whose gnarled boughs and slow-grown strength defy the climate, and which it seems a sacrilege to fell for firewood. But though the forests have much given way before human encroachment, they are safe for many years to come. The estate on which we stood is so richly provided with wood, that only

* Ten kopecks are equivalent to one penny.

an eightieth portion is yearly felled for building, firing, and other purposes, so that, by the time a third generation comes round to the division which the first cleared, another old forest is there before them.

One morning, for "*die Morgenstunde hat Gold im Munde*," I emerged at an earlier hour from beneath a muslin canopy which furnishes some protection from my tormentors, and drove by six o'clock to a wood five wersts off, accompanied only by my faithful attendant, who thrives uncommonly on the air and exercise she partakes with me. Our way led through dense woods of a younger growth, whose pliant boughs opened to the horses' heads and closed again after we had passed, and where, excepting the bush-ranger's cottage, which stood on a little island of meadow separating two mighty sweeps of forest, we left all signs of human habitation more than half-way behind us. Dismissing the droschky, we dived into the depths of one of these, nor stopped until completely hemmed in by a vast green-roofed cavern, supported on irregular pillars of every size and form;—some of them splendid erect monsters, who had never wavered in their sturdy course upwards—others slender drooping scions, falling in graceful lines across their veteran companions, as if demanding aid in the giddy ascent. This was a wood of mingled trees, the fresh hues of the oak contrasting with the black pines; and close to us stood a noble spruce, split from tip to base by the lightning of last week's storm—one half resting against a neighbouring stem—the other pale, bleeding, and still erect. Below lay forty feet of the luxuriant head, with enormous splinters, rent in longitudinal lines, while the ground was furrowed in deep angular troughs by the last strength of the fluid. Here was Heaven's doom dealt in a moment, but farther on lay the victims of slower thunderbolts; for the wood was strewn with cairns of moss-grown stones, through some of which the trees had forced their way, which showed where a plague-smitten body rested. There was something indescribably touching in this union of present life, movement, verdure, and luxuriance, with the reminiscences of human suffering and corruption; here and there the sun shooting across a silver birch trunk, like the light across a liquid human eye, or illuminating the red bark of a veteran Scotch fir with a fiercer glow, or stealing few and far between in slender bars of gold along the tender grass. But seldom did a short glance pierce to the bases of these giant stems, or visit the grave of the long-shunned and now long-forgotten sufferer.

Sounds were as scarce here as sunbeams— for in this birdless country no wing brushed the air, and no feathered throat swelled with melody; and only the distant bell of the straying cattle tinkled faintly at intervals through the covert. Our very voices startled us as we moved on through the mute activity of Nature; now sitting for hours on one green tuft, now seeking fresh pictures in the ever-varied repetition of this sylvan scene. And was the heart thus lonely thrown on Nature's sympathy? No; far from it—dear friends were thought of without that withering sense of separation which too often accompanies the noisier fellowship of a crowded room. Here, where there was nought to remind, all was calmly remembered, and memory opened her sad and sacred stores, free from the teasing importunities of harassing associations.

Other objects illustrative of the scenery of these woods are the number of ant-hills—not little mounds which a foot could disturb, but large and conical as a good-sized haycock— the ants themselves an inch long, on the same colossal scale as their dwellings. To erect these, the stump of a tree, here generally hewn three feet from the ground, is pitched upon, which, being gradually minced up into the finest particles by these indefatigable creatures, crumbles itself into a conical form, and with the accumulation of labour and life assumes the size I have described. Here the ants swarm in a red-black coating all the summer, and in winter retire deep within. They are harmless creatures, however, and carefully shunned us.

It was noon before the flight of time had been missed, and, alternately intent on my book, or gazing at the blue rents of sky which broke the dark mosaic of the branches overhead, the figure of my Sascha wandering up and down in a pensive attitude had been too perfectly in accordance with the scene to draw my attention; when, coming to my side, she falteringly owned to me the hopeless loss of—*her thimble*. Most pathetically did she aver that not above half a werst off she had it safe on her little round finger, counting for nothing, in her patient search, the millions of leaves and blades intervening, any one of which would effectually have concealed it. So there we left it to its hidden grave—a little atom of civilization dropped in the wild forest lap, to sink deeper and deeper beneath the alternate layers of snow and leaves of succeeding seasons,—and ourselves returned to the world whence we had come.

The day, commenced thus stilly, concluded in a large family-party at a neighbouring residence. By the word *family-party*, I must beg not to be understood one of those rude, indecorous gatherings—those social Babels of our native land, where brothers, sisters, cousins, nephews, and nieces meet together to banter, tease, and laugh; but an orderly meeting of courteous individuals, who know what befits their dignity, and are above taking advantage of the bonds of relationship to indulge in any promiscuous levity!—fie upon it! Even the very furniture partakes of the general feeling;—hard stuffed, bright polished, and richly carved, there is no indelicate straying about the rooms like our loose-mannered, depraved, forward generation, who come before they are called; but each stands austerely in its place, and waits to be sought. The ladies curtsey, the gentlemen bow, and sometimes a fair hand is reverently kissed, while the lady—for such is the peculiar custom both here and in Russia—is expected to dive down and imprint a chaste salute on the extreme confine of the cheek, or very tip of the ear, or any other part of the gentleman's physiognomy thus employed which her lips can reach. This requires some practice to do gracefully, for, what with impatience on the one hand and bashfulness on the other, or perhaps awkwardness on both, two heads have been known to come together harder than was quite agreeable.

Nevertheless this is looked upon by the gentlemen as their undoubted perquisite; and I have seen a pretty foreign woman gravely reprimanded by her dull Estonian lord for hesitating to comply. It would be hard to say what grade of relationship or exigency of circumstance would compel an Estonian nobleman to forget that he is not to be at his ease, according to our western notions of such. On the other hand, to a lover of antiquity, this living representation of by-gone manners is highly interesting. At every moment I am reminded of some trait which increasing luxury and increasing retrenchment have equally conspired to banish from our soil. Here every country gentleman keeps open house, and no account is taken of how many mouths there are to fill, whether in hall, kitchen, or stable. The houses are vast, grand, and incommodious, and countless hangers-on and dependants supply the economy of steps by a superfluity of feet. The Seigneurs here never move about with less than four horses, and often six,—rusty equipments, it is true;—but it is a mistake to imagine that the coaches and four of our ancestors were marked by the same neatness and finish which now attend the commonest pair; or that their neighbourly meetings were distinguished by that ease, sociability, and intellect which render the English society of the present day so delightful. On the contrary, as soon as the scanty topics of the day were exhausted, they all sat down to cards, and that perhaps by broad daylight, like too many of the Estonian gentlemen. Then, as now here, all natural products were plentiful and cheap, and all artificial objects scarce and dear; and the manners to correspond were hospitable in the main, but rigidly formal in detail. Manners, however, must be looked upon as an art, which, before it can be easy and safe, must be stiff and cautious—such are the necessary transitions of all other schools, and no less of this. In this light I respect these formal old worthies, whose study it seems equally to give me a hearty welcome and keep me at respectful distance, like the translated souls of my great grandfathers and grandmothers,—and take true delight in their venerable society; and if a profane weariness of mind and body do occasionally surprise me while sitting on a hard chair, and drilling my thoughts and figure to the starch standard of rectitude around me, be sure I ascribe it solely and entirely to my own corrupt condition, and to the incorrigible lolling propensities of my nature both moral and physical.

Another characteristic of this formal school, as worthy of imitation as note, is the fact that family quarrels are things utterly unknown here, and that none of that undue precedence is given to wealth as in countries more advanced. All those born in a certain station retain it, whether their means be adequate or not, and are admitted into society with no reference as to whether they can return the obligation. Otherwise I do not believe the real morality of the community in any way advanced by their rigid outward decorum. Like people who first peel their apple and then eat the paring, it comes to the same thing in the end. Consistent with the spirit of an old picture, they bend all their attention to the minutiæ of a fold, and neglect the first principles of perspective. Harmless freedoms are controlled with bars of iron, while, from the facility of divorce, and other laxities which the Lutheran religion allows, many a sin walks in broad daylight, without so much as a cobweb over it.

The class upon whom this prohibition of harmless freedoms, or in other words this chain upon natural spirits, falls heaviest, is that of the unfortunate little Estonian young ladies. Children of all ages are here palmed upon all society, greatly to mutual inconvenience. On entering a room full of company, the eye is caught by numbers of these half-way little women, with smooth tied hair and stiffened peaked figures, behung with gold brooches and ear-rings, and all the miniature paraphernalia of their mothers; who lead a miserable nomade life—wandering from room to room, with no place sacred from or to them; and are constantly being reminded, from four years of age and upwards, to be *weiblich*. If I held out my hand, they made me a disgusting little curtsey; if I ventured upon any approaches to play, they wondered what I was about. Oh! for the bright vision of a truly lovely English child, seldom seen and then cordially welcomed; who hastens forward to some grown-up playmate, trips over stools, turns up carpet-corners, and, arriving with ruffled locks and shortened breath, and with both her little hands fumbling in yours, can't at first perhaps utter a word for bashfulness! There may be some policy in breaking in children here thus early; but my heart bled for these little buckram countesses and baronesses, and I only trust that the moment our backs were turned they took to their heels and loosened all their little joints.

The conversation turned on the visit of the heir of Russia to England, and an ingenious little German romance was spun out by some grave grey-heads as to the probabilities of his falling in love with our Queen—her returning the flame—and the miseries of a hopeless passion; the piece ending with the grave question as to which of the august pair should renounce their inheritance. Of course it was soon decided which crown was to be abandoned, for the mere circumstance of a reigning queen is a sore point with the Estonians, who spend much virtuous indignation upon this supposed subversion of Nature's law, and are, I fear, prepared to hold their meek spouses with a tighter rein, lest forsooth they should follow the same example. Altogether many politic and wise provisions derived from our excellent constitution, which to us are truths familiar from childhood, are here made subjects of vehement altercation. The dignity and pre-eminence of our church—the law of primogeniture—the transmission of titles through the female line—the policy which preserves to a peeress her own dignity, be her husband the lowest commoner in the land—and the courtesy which permits every woman of rank upon marrying to retain the distinction of her birth, unless she merge it in a higher—are here all subjects which are submitted to the test of German reasoning, and declared unsound in the eye of Nature. Very erroneous notions are here also entertained as to the inordinate pride and undue prerogatives of the English nobility; forgetting that, when the titles and honours centre in one head only, the other members of the same family return to the middle walks of life, filling our professions with individuals whose sense of noble descent is the highest stimulus to honourable exertion; and who thus form a social link between the highest nobleman and the great body of the nation. And though far be the day when the English nobility should enjoy no prerogatives of birth, yet where can these be less galling than in that country where distinguished abilities may elevate any man to the highest offices in the state, and a sullied reputation keep any duchess from court? On this head no German may throw a stone at England. Earls without earldoms, barons without baronies; their titles unsupported by political consequence, and diluted to utter insignificance by the numbers who bear the same — their jealousy of rank increasing in proportion to its diminution,—no nobility hedges itself so carefully beneath a vexatious, trumpery spirit of exclusiveness, which is as absurd in itself as it is galling to those beneath them. In Russia no one may advance in the military service, in Estonia no one may purchase an estate, and in Weimar no one may enter the theatre by a particular door, who has not a *de* prefixed to his name; and these are only a few of the countless privileges with which they endeavour to bolster out an empty title, and exclude those who are often their betters in education, wealth, and refinement. As to that class of society peculiar to England—the aristocracy without title, the representatives of long-descended estates—the old squirearchy of the land, who often prefer the battered gold of their ancient family name to the bright brass of a new distinction,—this was a subject so incomprehensible, a paradox so preposterous, that for my own credit's sake I gave up the task of elucidating it.

Another subject of considerable interest discussed this evening was the gradual encroachment of Russian tendencies upon the German provinces, and the fear of a future consolidation with Russia, as well in manners as in allegiance. Nor is this apprehension groundless. These provinces, though possessed of an honourable internal administration, have never been able to maintain their own independence against the many competitors for them. Natural position assigns them to the dominion and protection of Russia; and the desire of generalising his system of government is as natural in the Emperor as that of retaining their nationality is in them. Their propinquity is in itself one main road to assimilation; and the late ordinances requiring the study of the Russian language in all schools, universities, &c., of these provinces, and establishing it as an article of examination prior to preferment, though met by much justifiable resistance, are not otherwise than fair, considering the number of Estonian and Livonian youths who find promotion in the civil and military services of Russia. On the other hand, it is the general remark that the best and most favoured officers in both these departments are drawn from these provinces. Another ordinance which particularly gives rise to murmurs is that compelling all children of a Russian parent, whether father or mother, to be of the Greek religion, *i. e.* so long as resident in Russia itself. From the frequent intermarriages of Estonians and Russians, this ukase has been more particularly the means of introducing Russian habits into the heart of Lutheran families. This may, however, be looked upon in an utterly different light, and, instead of encouraging the here deprecated march of union between the two countries, ought to act as a direct check. Those who now marry Russian wives do it with their eyes open as to the consequences; and as a regard for their own religion does not seem to counterbalance the temptation of a larger fortune than their Lutheran countrywomen can bring, no commiseration is due.

But now adieu to politics—the life in the forest under the greenwood tree is more to my taste.

LETTER THE TWENTIETH.

Fall and its beauties—The daughters of Fall—The Countess mother—A gathering of all nations—Cuisine—Occupations—Varieties of scenes and languages—The château—Its various treasures—Russian church—In-door beauties and out-door beauties—Count C. and Princess V.—Salmon-fishing—Illuminations—Adventurous passage—Countess Rossi—Armen-Concert at Reval—Rehearsals—The Scena from the Freischütz—Return home.

Who would imagine that this good, honest, fertile Estonia—this stronghold of old-fashioned decorum—this formal, straight-walked nursery of clipped thyme and rosemary—nourishes a pool of bitter waters in its centre, a traitor within its gates, a canker at its very root?—That in this precise, decorous province is reared a pavilion of luxury — a private theatre of fashion—a saloon of modern manners, owning no bounds but the invisible ring-fence of refinement, where all is ease, taste, expense, and indulgence—" all nature and all art?" Fall, the earthly name of this enchanted castle, is a residence in praise of whose natural beauties and artificial decorations everybody has expatiated to me since my domiciliation in this province. But accounts of beautiful scenery are so relative to the mind of the describer—so oft have I found *" une belle étable"* the standard of admiration here, while, on the other hand, my own taste, from sundry liberties it has taken in discovering beauties where, according to established rule and tradition, none had ever been known to exist, is become so very questionable, —that politeness on the one side now describes without one solitary hope of conversion, and politeness on the other now listens without one distant vision of gratification. But in the case of Fall I confess the wickedness of unbelief, and only wish I were oftener so punished. This is one of those favoured spots where Nature has compressed every imaginable beauty together, fitting them closer than, abstractedly considered, would be deemed pleasing; though, once presented to the view, criticism has nothing more to say.

Fall is in the possession of Count B., the man who, after the Emperor, wears the diadem in Russia. Here he has secured to his family a retreat from the world, or what might be so did not the world follow them faster than they can retreat;—in other words, a summer residence, where that most luxurious of all luxurious existences—one equally commanding the healthy gifts of the country and the lively gifts of the capital—is as well understood and practised as in our own land. A week spent in this charming spot is sufficient to make the evidence of the senses doubtful. It is not Estonia—that's quite sure; it is not Russia—here is no disorder; nor France—though the echoes answer in French numbers; nor England—though as like that as any. What is it, then? Where are you?—In beautiful, delicious, unique Fall—the garden of Nature—the *pot pourri* of all nations—the quintessence of all tastes; where the courtier, the philosopher, the lover of nature, the votary of fashion, the poet, the artist, the man of sense, or the man of nonsense, may all be happy in their own way.

Count B. was not unmindful of the effect and power of contrast in selecting a residence, for miles round which the eye is wearied by the monotony of one of the dullest and flattest plains in Estonia,—where even a river, that foil to all dull landscapes, sulks gloomily along, spreading itself over marshes it cannot beautify, and hiding itself behind rushes and sedges it cannot hide; till, viewing lofty banks rising in the distance, and graceful trees leaning pendent to caress it, it gathers its forces together, and cuts its way along with increasing willingness. And now all the beauties of an Alpine scene mirror themselves tremblingly on its ribbed and rapid surface, and light, airy bridges, fit for fairies' feet to cross, o'erleap it with their slender span,—and groves of blooming orange-trees, and every other incense-breathing flower, perfume its banks—and, in the gladness of his heart, the river-god flings himself, in a bound of joy, down a thundering cascade, rounding the edges of peaked and jagged rocks in a veil of oily transparency, and hiding their blackened bases in clouds of foam. Thence, dashing forward in many a changing, wreathing circle, its agitated fragments reflect for a moment the light Italian château, or ancient ruin, or classic temple,—or repeat in quivering lines the white flowing dresses and gay uniforms of some wandering group, till, gradually abating from its wild career, the stream winds heavier along, and, steering slower and slower to its final fate, quits the landscape, of which it had enhanced the every beauty, to spend its puny waters on the wide breast of the Baltic. From this cascade, or *fall*, the German name for this estate is derived; but the Estonian one of Yoala, though less significant, is more harmonious.

There is something in the air of Fall which gives beauty to every living thing on its surface. Owing to the position of the hills, and the vicinity of the sea, spring is here earlier, and autumn later, and all vegetation wears a correspondingly grateful aspect. Not only do the oak and beech flourish with English luxuriance, but trees foreign to this soil, the chest-

Ruin at Fall

nut, the sycamore, the plane, here abide the " bitter nip of frost;" while velvet lawns, green and fresh as the banks of Thames, encircle the bases of the high *Bergrücke*, or mountain-backs, or ridges, whose woods, assuming a more arctic nature as they stretch upwards, fence in this happy valley with a battalion of hardy pines. Nor may the beautifying influence of a Russian summer sky, which may defy comparison with any other in the world, be forgotten.

But why do I longer suppress what is foremost on my lips—why longer tamper with the irresistible desire to challenge any country, any clime, and any nurture, to produce fairer flowers of another and nobler kind than this fitting nursery has reared;—to throw the gauntlet to all the living generations in any known or unknown land, to outshine in beauty the peerless daughters of Fall? Woman's admiration of woman's beauty is more impartial than man's, and not less enthusiastic. Never shall I forget the first moment when these three exquisite creatures stood before me. The eldest, tall, straight, and slender as the glistening birch-stem on her own mountain-side; with skin of wax, and hair of gold lighting like an auréole round her delicately-formed head; and features and dimples like Hebe ere she knew disgrace, and a character of face of the highest aristocratic English style;—beautiful, in short, to her fingers' ends. And then the second, with her scarce nineteen summers, and matron-care already slightly resting on her marble brow, and yet a face like a vestal, with mild, pensive sentiment written on every chiselled feature—pale as alabaster, with tresses which seemed, by the weight of their massive coils, to bow down the stooping head and languid form. Lastly, that sweet youngest! as if Nature to make a third had joined the other two; with character more decided than her scarce ripened charms, and in both distinct from her sister beauties—with the mind to will, and the power to do; and a natural gift of penetration into others' thoughts, and secrecy over her own, lurking behind the loveliest, demurest, most transparent mask of tender beauty (true daughter of the man who knows and *keeps* all the secrets of Russia), which, unless a practised reader in physiognomy be greatly deceived, will make her the most fascinating and dangerous of the lovely trio. Of her an old diplomatist said—" *Jeune comme elle est, Mademoiselle Sophie a déjà le grand art de savoir paroître ce qu'elle veut?*"—a rich compliment in his coin; and, so long as the calm remains only in the exterior, and the warmth all within, a very safe one. Alas for those which my fancy had hitherto treasured as models of female beauty! fallen are your sceptres, broken are your crowns! Not even the gilding of remembrance, that natural cosmetic which the mind bestows on all absent favourites, can deck you in colours which may venture comparison with those before me. The world will see and hear of this lovely trefoil, whose charms will probably be transplanted to other countries; but Fall was their proper setting, and few will view them here united again.

These personal advantages are chiefly descended from the Countess-mother, a magnificent woman, with pride and pleasantry contending in her countenance—an Asiatic Mrs. Siddons, and still in the zenith of her charms; but the facial bond between mother and daughter is more of beauty than likeness.

Having no sons, the Count has entailed this residence upon his eldest daughter; but in Russia no entailed estate may descend to a foreigner, and Annette

> " Loves a knight from a far countrie,
> And her lands she will give for one glance of his e'e."

Fall therefore becomes the inheritance of the next sister, Princess V.

I arrived at Fall at a fortunate time. The last *pyroskaff* from Reval had just landed a little select colony of high life from Petersburg. There were princes with historical names, ministers with political names, and generals with military names. There was Count ——, the *richard* of Russia, who, " damned to wealth, buys disappointment at immense expense;" and the far-famed beauty, Madame K., whose perverse birth has proved no perversity to her at all; and Countess Rossi, charming and attractive as in her first burst of popularity, accompanied by her stately husband: with other beauties, and other talents and excellencies, both moral and titular; and stars flung on brave breasts by the Emperor of all the Russias,—and others (and oh, how far surpassing!) fixed in fair heads by the King of all kings.

For a private house in a remote province on the Baltic, we sat down daily to dinner as strange a collection of nations as can be imagined. There were Russians, Armenians, Germans, Italians, French, English, Swiss, and Dutch,—to say nothing of the various subdivisions of Estonian, Livonian, Austrian, Prussian, Bavarian,—more than I can remember; and last, and this time least, our ranks dwindled down to a dwarf, who strolled from saloon to ante-room just as he pleased. This was a memento of the olden time, which involuntarily brought with it fears of a corresponding barbarity. Ignatuschka, however, has at all events a happy time of it,—is no more of a buffoon than a shrewd wit, a talent for mimicry, and a due admiration for his own tiny proportions may make him, and is loved and cherished by every member of the family. So much so, indeed, that in sheer gratitude for good cheer and kind treatment, he has within the last few years, though already forty years of age, grown one inch! When all met together, French was the prevailing tongue; and when the groups scattered, each relapsed into their own. The *cuisine* was most costly; the groundwork French, with a sprinkling of incomprehensible native dishes, which I ate by faith only; and, in imitation of what here passes for English, half a sheep, or half a calf, which had fattened on the milk and honey of Fall, was brought in on a trencher by two staggering men-servants, while a renowned minister rose and bowed with mock humility to the steaming comer, and the Count, tucking a napkin over his stars and cordons, stood up and carved the beast,—and, to say the truth, had he hacked it with his sword, he would have done it as well.

The disposal of our time was much the same as with us in England;—in other words, each did as they wished. The Countess bore off a number to inspect her brilliant conservatories, almost a werst in length, her English dairy, &c.; and the Count headed a party of Dons, to view some important addition to his already forty measured wersts of serpentine paths, and rejoice their hearts with a new composition that *was* to have all the binding qualities of native English gravel; whilst the young and the pretty sat at their embroidery frames in the shade of cool marble terraces, or loitered round graceful vases, or stooped among flowers not fresher nor gayer than they.

Fall has been in the possession of Count B. for about fifteen years; and knowing the former proprietors to be as low in taste as high in worth, it frequently occurred to me what a burnishing this jewel had undergone in this short space of time. For, true to Estonian habits, the old mansion, the Countess assured me, was most curiously placed just where not one beauty of the landscape was visible. My host and hostess greatly regretted not having instituted a visitors' book at the first period of their occupation; for Fall had seen a succession of the noble and gifted, whose autographs would have been an heir-loom of price to future generations. A few years back the present Emperor and Empress honoured them with a visit, and were as much enraptured by the scenery as any of their subjects could be, —leaving a memento of their presence to descend to the future in a tree planted by each. The spades used by the Imperial hands are preserved, and inscribed with the date and occasion. Each is analogous to its wielder—the Empress's a fairy toy, the Emperor's only to be lifted by giant strength. Both the Count and Countess B. had lived through events of great historical interest: of the former more hereafter. The Countess had been twice married, having lost her first husband at the French invasion, when her house also was sacrificed in the destruction of Moscow. Often, in alluding to articles and souvenirs of her early youth, she added with a sigh, "They perished in the flames of Moscow."

Altogether, I never remember such mingled

and peculiar associations as I experienced in Fall. Here was one country within another—each as dissimilar as possible; and our every-day life made up of successive scenes of as many periods as nations. There were the Gothic halls, with every gorgeous appurtenance of alcove, stained glass, fretted pillar, oak carving, and mosaic floor; and a few old ladies sat in state in their high-backed chairs, or a couple of gentlemen strutted in the foreground in earnest pantomimic discussion. Then a prince, or general, hurried across the scene, and at the word " *Tchellovek*," or man, equivalent to the " What, ho!" of stage practice, in rushed two or three men-servants from the ante-room; and now and then a messenger, hard-ridden, arrived from court with secret tidings; and even the manners themselves, from the high rank of the individuals, and the occasional familiar handling of mighty names and weighty matters, though modern enough in other respects, wore a Shakspearian tone. And then the scene shifted, and a roaring water-fall, with Claude-like trees, appeared, and vistas of temples, crowned by the line of sea, and bright flowers or marble lions in front, with damsels in white with real roses in their hair. Or I stood before a mosque-like building, with gilded cupola; and a priest with flowing robe and high sorcerer's cap, and streaming hair and beard, mounted the steps; or a Russian vassal, with scarlet caftan, and Vandyke physiognomy, or a lowly Estonian peasant, with sandalled shoon, passed by. Or I was in a French boudoir, respiring nothing but modern luxury, with couches and curtains, and every gewgaw of ingenious idleness. The piece concluding most comfortably with an English bedroom, small, unostentatious, and private—everything, even to the Windsor soap on the wash-table, recalling those sanctuaries of home. No wonder, then, with French, German, Russian, and English alternately sounding around, that a simple individual was sometimes puzzled to know where the scene really lay.

The château of Fall itself is only appropriated to reception rooms and to the dwelling of the family, and is stored with all the mingled gorgeousness of Asiatic taste and the more polished art of European civilization. A magnificent collection of silver vessels of Oriental shape and purpose is a conspicuous object, and among the various treasures of art an enamel of Henry the Eighth with his six wives, magnificently set in silver, would be coveted by many an English collector. The accommodations for visitors consist in two houses on either hand set apart for that purpose—this being a custom prevalent both in Estonia and Russia. One of these houses, both of which were completely filled on the present occasion, joins on to the Russian church—a private edifice for the family, consecrated to St. Elizabeth, in honour of the Countess, being dedicated on her name's day. Here every Sunday, and on an occasional fête day, a Pope with deacons, choristers, and all their paraphernalia, are fetched from Reval, and generally begin their duties with a short mass on the Saturday eve. One of these I attended. The prohibition against sitting makes all Greek services very exhausting, and many a sincere believer in the *Vera*, as they particularly denominate their faith, shifted wearily from one foot to the other between the many and fatiguing obeisances which their Liturgy requires. All the family stood on a carpet before the screen which conceals the Holy of Holies, and behind them the household servants came and went, each addressing himself to a particular picture; and, since the number is their object, performing their genuflexions in double quick time. Amongst them I recognised my handmaiden hard at work, crossing and bowing; while, overlooking the difference of creed in their love of devotion, a few mild Estonian countenances peeped from the background. But "*Je reviens à mes premiers amours*"—beside me stood a figure, which once seen, my eye wandered to no other child of clay, or graven image around. It was Annette—more lovely than ever—her faultless face emerging from a bower of golden curls—her velvet and furs wrapped around her, betraying rather than concealing her exquisite symmetry; now folding her slender form down, like a fair flower surcharged with dew, till her waxen forehead touched the floor, now slowly rearing herself to her full height, and gaining new grace from the attitude of devotion. Oh! Annette, such an apparition as thou would, I fear, have disturbed my meditations in any place of worship. Whoever wins this bright being will own the fairest person, the sweetest voice, the blithest step and most cheerful mind that ever blessed mortal; and yet "a creature not too fair, or good, for human nature's daily food." Happiness is her atmosphere—the element in which she exists—anxiety seems as little intended for that gay temperament, as sentiment for that sunny face; and I doubt whether either would improve with the addition.

Never was poor mortal so taxed with an "*embarras de richesses pittoresques*" as myself. In-door beauties and out-door beauties assailed me at once, and no sooner had I fixed the one than my eyes played truant to the other. Before the sketch of some luxuriant landscape was half completed, I found myself sighing with longing glances at the group of fair recumbents who had cast themselves around me; with rich flowing and rustling garbs like a picture of Watteau, and minds, I fear me, no less in the spirit of his times. One lovely evening I shall never forget. I sat on one of the hanging spider-web bridges which a breeze could swing, and which a child's foot agitated too much for my pencil; all supernumerary gazers were therefore banished, and only Count C. remained half lying, half sitting on the one hand, and Princess V. on the other — he with all the confidence of a man long taught in the world, she with the double timidity of one who married from the school-room: so much so that had the whole varied little community been sifted through, two greater antipodes in character, both to be worthy and both to be wise, could hardly have been selected. For some time the conversation was not such as to turn my attention from the various angles of the château—the precise number of arched windows, and the alternate stripes of sunshine and

Château de Taill.

shade on wood and bank which were gradually being transmitted to my paper: when at length the discourse fell on coquetry; and to say the least, the woman must be deeply engrossed in the act itself who does not lend an ear to its discussion. I found matters running high. The Count, who, with his practised and polished tongue, and native wit, prides himself on sustaining a bad cause better than most a good one, was in full strain of eloquence extolling the praises of coquetry, and lording it unmercifully over the little vestal-faced and vestal-minded *Altesse*, whose straightforward arguments were twisted to his advantage as soon as uttered. In vain did she search her memory and all the fair ranks of her native capital for some instance of female attractiveness without this alloy, and in truth Petersburg, as I have since known it, was not the most promising covert for such a chase; till at length, in despair of a better, she exclaimed, "*Par exemple, moi, je ne suis pas coquette!*" "*Vous, Princesse! non, vous êtes charmante,*" said the courtier; "*mais vous êtes trop froide pour être coquette."* "*Pardonnez,*" rejoined the Princess, roused from her natural languor, and with a look which belied either his or her own assertion, "*la vraie coquette est la plus froide créature au monde.*" The Count was fairly beaten, and laid his arms laughing down, but capitulated on second thoughts with the stipulation that only "*une méchante coquetterie*" was reprehensible in either sex. In trifles such as this did these summer days of relaxation pass over; but trifles are the straws thrown on the current of human character, and fine lines are as sure to read by as coarse.

One night (for now the period was turned which led us slowly and relentlessly to winter's darkness) we were suddenly called out to witness the wild work of salmon fishing. It was a cloudy, moonless night; and issuing on the terrace, the dark valley before us looked for a moment like the starry firmament reversed on earth—every bridge, every path, every conspicuous object was studded with minute lamps, spangling the landscape without illuminating it. The summons, which was to the furthest bridge, just where the river stealthily seeks the sea, full two wersts off, called some from the piano, others from the card-table, and all unexpectedly. All was now confusion. Mantillas and kasavoikas were snatched from the colossal marble vase, where each flung her wrapper on entering the house, and the old ladies tied snug bonnets close under their chins to keep out the night air, and young ladies disposed light handkerchiefs or velvet hoods round their blooming faces, with not nearly so much caution, but incomparably more effect. In their hurry all the garden hats were missing. Now began a most disorderly march through the orange-scented and lamp-fringed paths; light enough to guide by, and yet dark enough to mistake by; and many a shoulder was tapped and hand touched by those who thought they saw a wife or sister in their muffled neighbour—for the mistake could not be voluntary!—while some very respectable bodies plodded on as if the scene had been the high road, and the time high noon-day, and here a straggler ran forward to startle the passers from behind some dark tree, and there a couple lagged behind, and seemed bent on anything but the right of precedence. Now, at a momentary pause of the buzz of whispering laughter, a bold voice loudly exclaimed, "*Point de coquetterie, Princesse,*" who, nestled close beneath her husband's cloak, was too confused at the novel charge to retort with better reason on her dauntless antagonist.

Then at a dark angle, where two paths fell together, a group of pretty lady's maids, bent on the same errand, mingled with our ranks before we had recognised the interlopers, or they their error; but "Honi soit qui mal y pense"—their native courtesy articulated itself in a few melodious Russian phrases, as they meekly drew back, and all was good humour. But I must except the unfortunate *richard*, who found the walk too much, or the excitement too little, for his habits, and returned. "*Monsieur s'ennuie partout*" was the low remark of a literary gentleman in his suite, and a sadder moral on inordinate wealth cannot be uttered. I'll be bound Ignatuschka is happier.

The scene brightened as we approached the river—the temples were illuminated—every tree wore a torch, and upon the river plied several boats with blazing firebrands for masts, while uncouth figures with brandished harpoons stood leaning intent over the fire-lit streaks and ripples of the otherwise black stream. These Neptunes were only meek Estonians, lighted and shaded into an aspect of ferocity, with their wild locks blown about with the wind, like the flames of the beacon above them, and throwing, as they passed to and fro in the boat, their huge shadows on the neighbouring banks, like shapeless phantoms hovering over the scene. We stood, a motley group, on a little wooden bridge which reaches zigzag from one huge rock to another over the stream. Nine fish were soon caught, and held aloft on their spikes; but nobody cared for the cruel sport, though none regretted the pleasant expedition. Returning home, the little lamps began to sink in their sockets and wish us good night; and some cynic,—not

Count C.,—exclaimed "*Le jeu ne vaut pas la chandelle,*" but nobody echoed him.

That same night a heavy thunderstorm cleared the air, and extinguished every lingering lamp; and the next morning the cascade presented itself before us in swollen magnificence and weightier peals—huge stones that the day before had emerged bare from the stream were now covered, and the zigzag bridge swept over by the torrent. But the air was cool and delicious, and the waters looked still more so; and—tell it not in Estonia—the pretty Sophie, forgetting her demureness, with another who looked no less wild than she really was, stripped off shoe and stocking, and were already half way upon the frail bridge, the water beating high against their white ankles, when a large party of us emerged in full view. Sophie shook her tiny fist at us as the rocks echoed to our applauses, but speed was impossible to the frightened girls.—Nor was the passage without danger; their footing was slippery, and the weight of water as much as they could resist, and, slowly labouring forward, we saw them set foot on dry land with great satisfaction. Gossamer pocket handkerchiefs were here apparently soon wetted through, and a peasant girl, barefooted like themselves, knelt down, and, with her petticoat of many colours, gently wiped off from those tender feet the sand and pebbles which her own did not feel; and then crossed the same bridge herself, with the addition of a heavy basket on her head, without exciting any one's interest.

And now let me revert more particularly to one of the fairest ornaments both in mind and person which our party possesses, whose never-clouded name is such favourite property with the public as to justify me in naming it—I mean the Countess Rossi. The advantages which her peculiar experience and knowledge of society have afforded her, added to the happiest *naturel* that ever fell to human portion, render her exquisite voice and talent, both still in undiminished perfection, by no means her chief attraction in society. Madame Rossi could afford to lose her voice to-morrow, and would be equally sought. True to her nation, she has combined all the *Liebenswürdigkeit* of a German with the witchery of every other land. Madame Rossi's biography is one of great interest and instruction, and it is to be hoped will one day appear before the public. It is not generally known that she was ennobled by the King of Prussia, under the title of Mademoiselle de Launstein; and, since absolute will, it seems, can bestow the past as well as present and future, with seven *Ahnherrn*, or forefathers—" or eight," said the Countess, laughing, " but I can't quite remember;" and though never disowning the popular name of Sonntag, yet, in respect for the donor, her visiting cards when she appears in Prussia are always printed *née de Launstein*. We were greatly privileged in the enjoyment of her rich and flexible notes in our private circle, and under her auspices an amateur concert was now proposed for the benefit of the poor in Reval. In this undertaking Countess Rossi and Prince V., of whom, if I have not spoken before, it is because I value him too highly to mention him trivially—were the representatives of treble and base, beneath whose banners a number of amateurs, with and without voices, soon ranged themselves. Some offered for music's sake, and others for fashion's sake; and parts were eagerly demanded by the *élite* among the bathing guests at Reval, as well as by a few practised singers belonging to a musical club among the *unadeliche*, or not noble, who unfortunately are the only class in Estonia who keep up any interest in such pursuits. These formed an excellent *fond* to keep wavering voices aright, for most of the fashionables thought chorus-singing would come by inspiration, and, when we all removed to Reval for the final rehearsals, were as innocent of their right parts as if they had never seen them. Madame Rossi, however, was the conscience as well as the organ of all the careless trebles: —no half-finished, slurred-over rehearsals were permitted. She stepped with courtesy and sweet temper from one tuneless group to another, bearing the right note aloft till all clung securely to it, and was never weary of helping and hearing. The opening chorus was "*die Himmel erzählen die Ehre Gottes,*" or the well-known "Heavens are telling," from the Creation;—Henzelt, the celebrated pianist, whom accident had brought to Reval, a man of exquisite finger and most interesting exterior, conducting the whole from the piano.

But these ladies were worse to teach than charity-girls. Some of them deemed the rehearsals utterly superfluous, others left their parts behind them, and others were so inveterately in good humour that it was difficult to scold them for being as much out of tune. Of one pretty creature with more animation in her face than music in her soul, whose voice in the Creation wandered to forbidden paths, a Russian humorist observed, "*Elle chante des choses qui n'ont jamais existé, même dans la Création !*"

Altogether these rehearsals were merry meetings, and when our own bawling was over Madame Rossi went through her songs as scrupulously as the rest. I shall never forget the impression she excited one evening. We were all united in the great ball-room at the Governor's castle in Reval, which was partially illuminated for the occasion, and, having wound up our last noisy "*Firmament,*" we all retreated to distant parts of the salle, leaving the Countess to rehearse the celebrated Scena from the Freischütz with the instrumental parts. She was seated in the midst, and completely hidden by the figures and desks around her. And now arose a strain of melody and expression which thrills every nerve to recall —the interest and pathos creeping gradually on through every division of this most noble and passionate of songs,—the gloomy light,—the invisible songstress,—all combining to increase the effect, till the feeling became almost too intense to bear. And then the horn in the distance, and the husky voice of suppressed agony whilst doubt possessed her soul, chilled the blood in our veins, and her final burst, "*Er ist's, Er ist's,*" was one of agony to her audience. Tears, real tears, ran down cheeks both fair and rough, who knew not and cared not that they were there; and not until the excitement had subsided did I feel that my wrist had been clenched in so convulsive a grasp by my neighbour as to retain marks long after the siren had ceased. I have heard Schröder and Malibran, both grand and true in this composition, but neither searched the depths of its passionate tones, and with it the hearts of the audience, so completely as the matchless Madame Rossi.

On the evening preceding the concert a public rehearsal was held at half price, which gave the finishing stroke to the choruses; and, as far as the principals were concerned, was just as attractive as the concert itself. Suffice it to say that this latter went off with great éclat, and anybody who may have occasion to examine the Petersburg Gazettes of the time will find a florid account of its success, together with the names of all the noble individuals concerned therein. It realised 4500 roubles, which, from the circumstance of the crown's having *forgotten* to pay its yearly donation of 1000 roubles to the chief charitable institution, and there being a little ill-timed delicacy in high quarters as to the policy of a reminder, was doubly welcome.

The Countess was greatly exhausted, and languor stole on all the party as we returned to Fall, whose woods and streams looked fresher than ever. The next day I quitted this paradise of mingled sweets and returned with unaltered zest to my quiet home, and with increased enjoyment to that being whose smile of beauty and whose voice of love had that superiority over those I had quitted, that my heart could never find words to describe either the one or the other.

LETTER THE TWENTY-FIRST.

Autumn scenes—Separation from Estonia.

The beauties of autumn, and the moral of its yellow leaves, are seen and felt in all countries. Nowhere, however, I am inclined to think, can the former be so resplendent, or the latter so touching, as in the land where I am still a sojourner. In our temperate isle autumn may be contemplated as the glorious passing away of the well-matured—the radiant death-bed of the ripe in years—while here the brilliant colours on earth and sky are like the hectic cheek and kindling eye of some beautiful being whose too hasty development has been but the presage of a premature decay. Thus it is that the vast plains and woods of Estonia are now displaying the most gorgeous colours of their palette, ere the white brush of winter sweep their beauties from sight, while the golden and crimson wreaths of the deciduous trees, peeping from amongst the forests of sober pines, may be compared to gay lichens sprinkling their hues over a cold grey rock, or to a transient smile passing over the habitual brow of care.

But all too hasty is the progress of this splendid funeral march—even now its pomp is hidden by gloomy slanting rains, its last tones lost in the howl of angry blasts, which, as if impatient to assume their empire, are rudely stripping off and trampling down every vestige of summer's short-lived festival, while Nature, shorn of her wealth, holds out here and there a streamer of bright colours, like a bankrupt still eager to flaunt in the finery of better days.

This season, as the dismal forerunner of that time which is to sever me from Estonia and all its real and acquired bonds of attachment, is doubly autumn to me. Whatever you do or see, says Dr. Johnson, consciously for the last time, is ever accompanied by a feeling of regret. How just then the sorrow of one who has found a second home in the land she now must quit! Cowards die a thousand deaths ere the dreaded stroke arrive, and affection, which can nerve itself for every trial save that of separation, suffers a thousand partings ere the final wrench ensue. But where is the remedy? The heart that deepest feels will also keenest anticipate. In occasions of joy, this is too often the better part;—would it were the worst with those of sorrow.

It is easy abstractedly to reason upon and even to make light of the privileges of mere local vicinity—of mere temporary union—as compared with the ubiquity of affection's thoughts, and the perpetuity of the heart's fidelity. It is easy to say that all earthly light must have its shadow—that the race is not to the swift, nor the battle to the strong—that few abide with those with whom they for ever would stay:—this is all very easy, too easy, to say. But what do such arguments avail when you awake each morning with an undefined sense of impending evil—when your days are spent as if the sword of Damocles hung suspended over your head, and when each separation for night tells you that another day has passed away of the few still left! Where is all your firmness when you hear the music of a light footstep, or feel the touch of the gentle hand which rouses you at once from your reveries of forced philosophy, and dissipates all its resolutions! Or, worst of all, when at some sign of approaching separation—at some allusion to a future to be spent apart—you see an eye, heavy laden, turn hastily away, as if to punish itself for a weakness which threatens to overset your strength! No—such feelings as these admit of no reasoning—the conflict is worse than the surrender. The affections in general may most require guidance, but there are seasons when they are the best law to themselves, when the wisdom of the world is utter foolishness with them.

How countless are the numbers and various the tongues of those who have written and sung of that love, evanescent when favoured, wretched when opposed, which binds man and woman! But who has told of the depths of that feeling which leads neither to selfishness nor to shame, which is neither maintained by art nor endangered by change—who has traced the course of that sweet fountain of poetry which flows steadiest on through banks of the deadliest prose — the affection which unites two sisters!—This is the only earthly love which has cast out fear—which takes nought amiss—loses no moments in misunderstanding—which knoweth no jealousy save the jealousy of the loved one's sufferings—which would sacrifice even her love rather than she should need yours—which has all the tenderness, the delicacy, the sensitiveness of the other passion—all its beauty and none of its barbarity; which is always in the honeymoon of love's kindness, without the vulgarity of love's satiety; which compensates where it cannot defend, sympathises where it cannot help— * * *

But let this subject pass: it is one too sacred for exhibition, too delicate for analysis;—those who know its blessings will also understand its penalties.

Nor is this all: the traveller who ventures

to bide that time when the force of old habits and associations can no longer impede the entrance of new preferences must prepare for many regrets; for, ere we suspect the deed, the heart is found to have thrown out numberless slender fibres into the new soil around, all painful to divide. When I first entered Estonia, it was with the laudable resolve, easier made than kept, of investing no feeling, of forming no friendship in the foreign world here opened to me, but of rigidly restricting all present happiness and future regret to that one being who I knew would furnish both in overflowing measure. But what knows the heart about systems of policy! Had the social atmosphere been rude, or the social elements repelling, it would have cost the traveller no effort to wrap her mantle of reserve close about her; but when the sun of kindness shone ceaseless forth,—when every avenue to susceptibility was besieged with gentle courtesies and gratuitous hospitalities—what remained but to throw it off and surrender a willing prisoner?

Were I to enumerate all those who not only met but sought that stranger who came coldly determined not to love, but was not proof to being loved, with a kindness as much above her deserts as beyond her powers of requital, it would fill a letter more interesting to her than any that has gone before. Suffice it to say that those who were rich in this world's gifts have treated the traveller with a simple and sincere heartiness, without which all the luxury of their princely residences would have attracted no feeling save that of curiosity; while those who were out of suits with Fortune have welcomed her to humble homes, where the utmost refinement of mind and polish of acquirement have furnished a charm money could not have bought.

It is with a heavy heart that I prepare to bid farewell to Estonia. Its past history is now familiar to those who may scan these letters, and its future destinies must be interesting speculation to those who would desire to see so many fine elements improved to their utmost. The tendencies of this province are all markedly German. To compel the substitution of Russian would be to compel it to retrograde. It cannot rebel. All violation, therefore, of those terms by which Russia originally made the acquisition of these provinces—all interruption of that independence of administration and liberty of action which were the conditions of their surrender, merely because they are unable to enforce them—would be as unfair as unwise.

From the stability of this vast empire the Baltic provinces derive protection and peace; but in their turn they hold out a model of simplicity and integrity in the administration of justice, which, in Russia, cannot be termed obsolete, but rather unknown. At the same time there is ample space for the exercise of obedience and the pride of independence;— ample means for giving Cæsar the things that are Cæsar's, without defrauding or selling their own nationality.

Fairly considered, the position of the Estonian noble is one of the happiest that man can desire. He enjoys the privileges of rank and importance without its fatigues—the blessings of independence without its responsibilities. His sphere of usefulness is wide—his means of existence easy. It rests only with himself to unite the refinements of education with the healthiness of a country gentleman's life. He has it infinitely more in his power to promote the welfare of his little, fertile, favoured province, than the Russian government has at present inclination to thwart it.

It is impossible to guarantee the maintenance of a nation's or of a province's prosperity where there is no constitutional pledge for safety; but, as things now stand; there is less to be feared in Estonia from the caprices of the crown than from the influence of individuals, who do not scruple to wrong their countrymen in the futile attempt to propitiate power.

LETTER THE TWENTY-SECOND.

Russia considered as a study—New-Year's Eve—Peculiar family demonstrations—Bridge of Kisses—Routine of a Petersburg life—Oriental regiments, and Oriental physiognomy—Fête at the Winter Palace—Scene from the gallery of the Salle Blanche—Court costume—Display of diamonds—Masked ball at the theatre—The Emperor —The Heritier—The Grand Duke Michael—Masked ball at the Salle de Noblesse—Uses and abuses of masked balls in Russia.

Petersburg, January.

This change of place has brought with it such a corresponding change of outward life, that to continue these letters in the same unbroken form would be impracticable. Although living in the centre of Russian society, and exposed at every pore to its influences, yet my impressions of those characteristics which distinguish it from other countries can be gleaned only in irregular succession, and in such only rendered again. Of all the states in the world, Russia is at this time most particularly that which requires the application of principles grounded equally on the studious knowledge of the past and a lucid judgment of the future to render that wholeness and impartiality of opinion which may be comprehensible to others and just to her. Those who would fairly judge Russia must first strip themselves of those habits of thought which, whatever their seeming, are only coincident with the age to which they have the accident to belong, and go back to those raw but stable elements which are the sole groundwork for a nation's prosperity, and which, in the present turmoil of hasty and changing opinions, have little chance of being comprehended and appreciated save by some old-fashioned representative of an old-fashioned country, who considers the a, b, c of loyalty and obedience the sole basis of any safe knowledge and of any solid civilization.

The two species of writers who have hitherto made Russia the subject of their pens are either the mere tourist, who sees and judges as the passing traveller—or those whom public office or private connection has thrown into the highest circles of the capital, and are thus placed where they may, it is true, analyse the froth, but are far from reaching the substance of the nation. No one has hitherto attempted the *philosophy* of this country, than which no subject to reflecting and generalising minds can be more interesting; while those dissertations on its political aspect which have appeared in our periodicals are so coloured with obvious partiality, or with obvious invective, as rather to deter the reader from forming any distinct opinion than to give him any premises whereon to rest.

Russia has only two ranks—the highest and the lowest; consequently it exhibits all those rudenesses of social life which must be attendant on these two extreme positions of power and dependence. It is vain therefore to look for those qualities which equally restrain the one and protect the other, and which alone take root in that half-way class called forth in the progress of nations equally for the interest of both. For in this light it is impossible to view the scanty and broken-linked portion of Russian society which a sanguine and too hasty policy has forced, not nourished, into existence, and which at present rather acts as the depression and not the foundation of that most important body denominated the middle ranks of a nation. To study the real destinies of Russia the philosopher of mankind must descend to a class still in bondage, and not yet ripe for freedom, but where the elements of political stability and commercial energy are already glaringly apparent.

As I may include myself among the second class of Russian travellers above mentioned, it is needless to state that it is as little in my power as in my inclination to enter upon subjects requiring equally difference of position and superiority of capacity, or rather no further than as they may be indirectly connected with the habits of the highest circles; if indeed so fragile a key may in any way be applied to the ponderous internal machinery of a state like Russia.

I entered Petersburg at a season particularly enlivened by festivities—viz. at the end of December (old style); and my first introduction into domestic scenes may be said to have commenced with the eve of New-year's Day. On this occasion every member near and remote of a large family connection, to the number of at least forty, assembled in the magnificent apartments of Count ——'s hotel. The evening passed away most cheerfully, and towards midnight we all paired off to supper. Here every delicacy was spread, and champagne poured out freely; but as the hour which dismissed the old and installed the new year resounded from the great clock on the staircase, every one rose, glass in hand; and now commenced a scene in which old and young—old men and children, young men and maidens—all took a share, and which, however matter-of-fact to relate, was highly amusing to witness. In plain language, then, everybody present kissed everybody present—one unrelated head, I beg to observe, excepted. This ceremony occupied some time, since, according to vulgar calculation, not less than sixteen hundred kisses were on this occasion exchanged.—Not hasty, piano, shamefaced commissions, but fearless, powerful, resounding salutations which left no question of the fact—

more noisy, however, than mischievous, more loud than deep—in many cases the cheeks of the parties being simultaneously presented, and the kiss lost on the desert air. It was very amusing to see the crowd as they circulated together—the silence only broken by the jingling of glasses and the very audible nature of their occupation. After which evaporation of family affection the whole party resumed their seats and continued their meal.

This is the national salute—in universal vogue from remote antiquity—rather a greeting than a caress—derived equally from religious feeling and from Oriental custom. Fathers and sons kiss—old generals with rusty moustachios kiss—whole regiments kiss. The Emperor kisses his officers. On a reviewing day there are almost as many kisses as shots exchanged. If a Lilliputian corps de cadets have earned the Imperial approval, the Imperial salute is bestowed upon the head boy, who passes it on with a hearty report to his neighbour; he in his turn to the next, and so on, till it has been diluted through the whole juvenile body.

If the Emperor reprimand an officer unjustly, the sign of restoration to favour as well as the best atonement is—a kiss. One of the bridges in Petersburg is to this day called the *Potzalui Most*, or Bridge of Kisses [not of Sighs], in commemoration of Peter the Great, who, having in a fit of passion unjustly degraded an officer in face of his whole regiment, kissed the poor man in the same open way upon the next public occasion on this very bridge.

On a holiday or *jour de fête* the young and delicate mistress of a house will not only kiss all her maid-servants but all her men-servants too; and, as I have mentioned before, if the gentleman venture not above her hand, she will stoop and kiss his cheek. As for the Russian father of a family, his affection knows no bounds: if he leave his *cabinet d'affaires* ten times in the course of the morning and enter his lady's saloon above, he kisses all his family when he enters, and again when he leaves the room: sometimes indeed so mechanically, that, forgetting whether he has done it or not, he goes a second round to make all sure. To judge also from the number of salutes, the matrimonial bond in these high circles must be one of uninterrupted felicity — a gentleman scarcely enters or leaves the room without kissing his wife either on forehead, cheek, or hand. Remarking upon this to a lofty-looking creature who received these connubial demonstrations with rather a suspicious sang-froid, she replied, "*Oh! ça ne veut rien dire—pour moi, je voudrais tout autant être battue qu'embrassée —par habitude!*"

The Russians have from long practice acquired such a facility in this respect, that a quick succession of salutes is nearly equal in power of intonation to the clapping of hands. It must be very fatiguing! But now—

> "As a surfeit of the sweetest things
> The deepest loathing on a nature brings"—

it may be as well to quit this subject.

The daily routine of a Russian family of this rank is easily complied with. Breakfast no visitor is expected to join; the family usually assembling for this meal in too deep a négligé for a stranger to witness. By noon the lady of the house is seated at her writing-table or embroidery-frame. Lunch is not served, but each orders a hot cutlet as he may feel inclined. Then visitors throng in, or the carriage and four awaits you, for here wheels are deemed the most becoming conveyance for age and dignity, although youth and beauty are seen gliding through the noiseless streets in open sledges. This mixture of vehicles, however, cuts up the snow, which here, from the severity of the frost and the restless traffic, lies in the principal street in ridges of fine crystals—like sand both in colour and quality—and is very heavy for the horses. Dinner is generally at four—at least, this is the Imperial hour; and as the Imperial movements are all rapid, and no one is expected to stay after dinner, our host frequently returns from dining with his Majesty in time for his own five o'clock repast, which not unseldom he pronounces the better of the two. After dinner the more intimate friends of the family drop uninvited in, and make up the whist-table; and then some depart for the theatre, or later for balls, and so the days go round.

But to return. It was New-year's Day, and, having taken my solitary breakfast, I was seated at my occupations, when a jingle of spurs was heard at my door, and Prince B—— entered the room to apprise me that detachments from the Circassian, Kirghise, and other Oriental regiments, *pour féliciter* the Count, were below in full uniform. Snatching therefore a mantilla from the hands of Sascha, whose Reval ideas were rather disturbed by the intrusion of a pair of epaulettes in my sanctuary, I hastily followed to the ante-room of the Count's cabinet, and stood between a file of soldiers drawn up in opposite lines. They were armed to the teeth—swords, pistols, cutlasses, bows and arrows; their powder-charges ranged six on each breast; their uniform red, with a casque of chain mail fitting close round the face and descending on the shoulders, with numerous other appendages for which my European ideas discovered neither use nor name; terminating with red Turkish slippers pointed upwards— altogether a most striking and martial dress.

But if their accoutrements were fierce, their looks corresponded. Not a blue nor a grey eye

—not a soft, nor a calm, nor a sleepy look was to be discerned, but a row of burning black lenses flashed on the stranger who had ventured within the range of their focus. We erroneously impute the beauty of languor to the Circassian physiognomy. Here there was no smothered fire, no veiled beams,—every face blazed with a restless glow. The features were regular—the complexions dark; but this red-hot expression defaced all beauty. They were all small men—the officers taller than the privates, but with the same inflammable character of physiognomy. These latter had acquired the French language, and were courteous and graceful in manner.

By noon of the same day I was summoned to accompany my kind hostess and her beautiful daughter, who as Dame and Demoiselle d'honneur attended at the celebration of the New-year's fête at the Winter Palace. There was no military *spectacle*, the weather being too severe; for reviews are not willingly undertaken if the thermometer be below 10°. The *Grande Place* before the Imperial entrance was thronged with carriages and sledges of every description, and guarded by troops of soldiers. We entered this superb palace, so late a mere burnt-out crust, and, leaving my two gorgeously attired companions to pursue their way to the Imperial presence, I was conducted by Prince V., in his glittering chamberlain's dress, upstairs and through corridors, all smelling of recent building and fresh paint, and placed by him in an advantageous position in the gallery above the Salle Blanche—the most magnificent apartment in this most magnificent of palaces, and so called from its decorations being all in pure white relieved only with gilding. Eighty feet below me in miniature size was a splendid pageant. Ranged along the walls stood a triple row of motionless soldiery; on one side, in graceful contrast with their stiff lines, was congregated a fair bevy of female figures, with sweeping trains and gleaming jewels; while slim figures of court chamberlains, with breast and back laden with the richest gold embroidery, with white pantaloons and silk stockings, hurried across the scene—or stopped to pay homage to the ladies—or loitered to converse with the groups of officers in every variety of uniform, with stars, orders, and cordons glittering about them, who sauntered in the centre. Conspicuous among these latter was the person of the Grand Duke Michael, brother to the Emperor—a magnificent figure, with immense length of limb and a peculiar curve of outline which renders him recognisable at any distance, among hundreds in the same uniform, and who was seen pacing slowly backwards and forwards on the marble-like parquête, and bending fierce looks on the soldiery.

Nor was the scene above without its attractions and peculiarities, for many distinguished-looking individuals were leaning over the same railings with myself—among them an Ingrelian princess—a middle-aged woman of uncommon beauty, with commanding features and long languishing eyes, and a peculiar high head-dress, flowing veil, and a profusion of jewels. And at the upper end, apart from all, sat in a solitary chair the Grand

Duchess Olga, second daughter of the Emperor, a most beautiful girl of sixteen, just restored from a dangerous fever, the traces of which were visible in the exquisite delicacy of her complexion, and in the light girl-like cap worn to hide the absence of those tresses which had been sacrificed to her illness. She was attended by her preceptress, Madame Baranoff.

But now the drums beat, the trumpets sounded, and every eye turned below. A cortège was seen advancing through the open entrance, and the Commandant Sakachefsky, rearing his full length and corpulent person, put himself with drawn sword at their head. A line of military passed; then a body of chamberlains,—when the band broke into the soul-stirring national hymn "*Boje Zara chrani*" —the troops presented arms, and a noble figure was seen advancing.

This was the Emperor—the plainest dressed, but the most magnificent figure present, wanting no outward token to declare the majesty of his presence. He passed slowly on, accommodating his manly movements to the short feeble steps of the Empress, who, arrayed in a blaze of jewels, dragged a heavy train of orange-coloured velvet after her, and seemed hardly able to support her own weight. To the Imperial pair succeeded the *Naslednik*, or *Heritier*, the slender prototype of his father's grand proportions,—with the Grand Duke Michael, and the youngest son of the Imperial house. Portly ladies and graceful maids of honour, with grey-haired generals, were seen in glistening train behind. But the eye followed that commanding figure and lofty brow, towering above every other, till it vanished beneath the portals leading to the chapel. And now ensued all the disorderly rear of a procession—tardy maids of honour and flirting officers, who came helter-skelter along, talking and laughing with a freedom proportioned to their distance from the Imperial pair—till the doors closed on them also, and the immovable military were left to thank the gods that the Grand Duke's eyes were otherwise employed.

And now my kind chamberlain again appeared; and, in order to avoid an apartment where the Grand Duchesses were stationed, we made the circuit of the palace, up stairs and down stairs—a walk which occupied more than ten minutes—and returned to within a short distance of my former position, to a window overlooking the chapel. Here stood the whole cortège thickly compressed together— one blaze of diamonds, stars, and epaulettes— while in advance of the rest was the Imperial family; the Empress, on account of her ill health, alone seated; the Emperor on her right, motionless as a statue; the Naslednik on her left, shifting from one long limb to the other—all crossing themselves and bowing at intervals. The service lasted two hours, varied only by the delicious responses of the court choristers. It was performed by the metropolitan and two other dignitaries of high rank, in high wizard caps and gorgeous mystic robes, who looked like the priests of Isis, or any other theatrical representation of sacerdotal dignity. After this the procession returned as it came.

The Empress detained the ladies for chocolate and refreshments; and the countess and

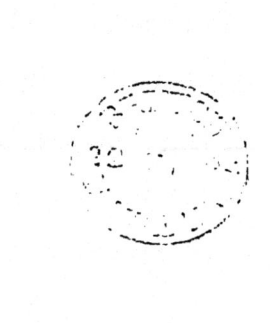

Demoiselle d'honneur

her daughter returned home perfectly exhausted with the duties of the day.

The court costume is both magnificent and becoming. It has been introduced in the present reign, and consists of a white satin dress fastened up the front with gold buttons, and richly embroidered in gold with a graceful Grecian pattern. Over this is a velvet robe, green for the Dames d'honneur, crimson for the Demoiselles, with long hanging sleeves, and descending in an ample train worked all round with a gorgeous scroll of wheat-ears in gold. The head-dress agrees in shape with the common national costume—being what is termed a *pavoinik*, a fan-shaped machine—orange velvet for the Dames d'honneur, and any dark colour they please for the Demoiselles,—closed at the back of the head for the former, and open for the latter, with a long blond veil attached, which flows half way down the dress. This *pavoinik* is laden with as many diamonds as it can carry; and as the Empress's recollections of *toilette* are excessively tenacious, care is taken to appear every time in a new device, and to vary the form and position of the diamonds, which, to compare things vile with things precious, all unhook for this purpose like the cut crystals of a chandelier. The neck and arms are also adorned with corresponding brilliancy.

The display of diamonds here is immense. Every woman of rank has a glass case, or a succession of glass cases, like those on a jeweller's counter, where her jewels are spread out on purple velvet, under lock and key, in her own bedroom; and as it is here that she often receives her morning guests, for nothing is seen of sleeping or dressing apparatus save the superb mirrors and a gorgeous screen, her wealth of brilliants and other jewels is displayed to advantage. Here also, in the jewel-case of the high-born matron, lies the miniature of the Empress, ornamented with brilliants, the insignia of the Dame d'honneur. Likewise, with those who are so honoured, the Order of St. Catherine, no less resplendent with diamonds; while in the young ladies' display, side by side with necklaces and bracelets, may generally be found the *chiffre*, or initial of the Empress, an A. in diamonds, which denotes the Demoiselle d'honneur. The number of these latter is at this time about a hundred and fifty.

On the 6th of January, O.S., the fête of the three kings, this court ceremony was renewed, with the addition of a procession of priests. After which the Emperor proceeded to bless the waters of the Neva, which are supposed to be gifted with supernatural virtues; on which occasion himself and everybody present is bareheaded. The severity of the weather and the amount of the crowd forbade any attempt to witness this national ceremony.

I was now becoming impatient for a nearer view of that awful personage whom all united in describing as "*le plus bel homme qu'on puisse s'imaginer*," and who, whether seen from the diminishing heights of the Salle Blanche,—or dashing along, his white feathers streaming, and muffled in his military cloak in his solitary sledge with one horse,—or striding with powerful steps, utterly unattended, in the dusk of the early evening, the whole length of the Nevski, wore a halo of majesty it was impossible to overlook. An opportunity for a closer view soon presented itself.

It was Sunday; and, after attending morning service at the English Church—the more impressive from long privation of its privileges,—I was driving, twelve hours later, viz. at midnight, with Princess B. and Countess L., to a very different resort—namely, to the great theatre, where, after the dramatic performances, masquerades are held once or twice a-week before Lent. These are frequented by a mixed public, the Salle de Noblesse being reserved for the disguise of the individuals *de la plus haute volée:* these latter therefore on occasions like this take a box on a level with the floor of the theatre, which extends on these nights over the whole of the parterre, and thus participate without actually mixing in the scene.

The coup d'œil on entering the box was very striking. A multitude of several hundreds was gathered together in the theatre's vast oblong; the women alone masked, and almost without exception in black dress and domino; the men, and those chiefly military, with covered heads and no token of the occasion save in a black scarf, as sign of domino, upon their left arm—their white plumes and gay uniforms contrasting vividly with the black-faced and draped figures around them; all circulating stealthily to and fro; no music, no dancing, no object apparent but gesticulation, whisper, mystery, and intrigue.

Here a knot of witch-like figures, as if intent on mischief, stood muttering in low tones together. There a slight mask tripped up to a stately grave general, tapped his shoulder, and, passing her arm into his, bore him off with significant nods. In front of us a couple of these sibyls, with bright eyes gleaming through their gloomy masks, attacked a young officer in high, squeaking, counterfeit tones, laughing and jeering, while the good man looked bewildered from the one to the other, and seemed to say, "How happy could I be with either!" And farther, apart from the throng, sat on a low step a solitary mask, who shook her head solemnly at all who approached, as if awaiting some expected prey;—while, half timid, half coquette, a light figure whispered some words in a gentleman's ear, and then, retreating before his eager pursuit, plunged into the crowd, and was lost to his recognition among the hundreds of similar disguises.

The Heritier, the Grand Duke Michael, the Duke de Leuchtenberg, were all seen passing in turn—each led about by a whispering mask —"*Mais où est donc l'Empereur?*" "*Il n'y est pas encore*" was the answer; but scarce was this uttered when a towering plume moved, the crowd fell back, and enframed in a vacant space stood a figure to which there is no second in Russia, if in the world itself; —a figure of the grandest beauty, expression, dimension, and carriage, uniting all the majesties and graces of all the Heathen gods,—the little god of love alone perhaps excepted,—on its ample and symmetrical proportions. Had this nobility of person belonged to a common *Mougik* instead of to the Autocrat of all the Russias, the admiration could not have been less, nor scarcely the feeling of moral awe. It was not the monarch who was so magnificent a man, but the man who was so truly imperial.

He stood awhile silent and haughty, as if disdaining all the vanity and levity around him, when, perceiving my two distinguished companions, he strode grandly towards our box, and, just lifting his plumes with a lofty bow, stooped and kissed the princess's hand, who in return imprinted a kiss on the Imperial cheek; and then leaning against the pillar remained in conversation.

The person of the Emperor is that of a colossal man, in the full prime of life and health; forty-two years of age, about six feet two inches high, and well filled out, without any approach to corpulency—the head magnificently carried, a splendid breadth of shoulder and chest, great length and symmetry of limb, with finely formed hands and feet. His face is strictly Grecian—forehead and nose in one grand line; the eyes finely lined, large, open and blue, with a calmness, a coldness, a freezing dignity, which can equally quell an insurrection, daunt an assassin, or paralyse a petitioner; the mouth regular, teeth fine, chin prominent, with dark moustache and small whisker; but not a sympathy on his face! His mouth sometimes smiled, his eyes never. There was that in his look which no monarch's subject could meet. His eye seeks every one's gaze, but none can confront his.

After a few minutes his curiosity, the unfailing attribute of a crowned head, dictated the words, "*Kto eta?*"—"Who is that?"—and being satisfied—for he remarks every strange face that enters his capital—he continued alternately in Russian and French commenting upon the scene.

"*Personne ne m'intrigue ce soir*," he said: "*je ne sais pas ce que j'ai fait pour perdre ma réputation, mais on ne veut pas de moi.*" As he stood various masks approached, but, either from excess of embarrassment or from lack of wit, after rousing the lion, found nothing to say. At length a couple approached and stood irresolute, each motioning the other to speak. "*Donnez-moi la main*," said a low trembling voice. He stretched out his noble hand: "*et voilà l'autre pour vous*," extending the other to her companion; and on they passed, probably never to forget the mighty hand that had clasped theirs. Meanwhile the Emperor carefully scanned the crowd, and owned himself in search of a mask who had attacked him on his first entrance. "*Quand je l'aurai trouvé, je vous l'amènerai;*" and so saying he left us.

I watched his figure, which, as if surrounded with an invisible barrier, bore a vacant space about it through the thickest of the press. In a short time a little mask stepped boldly up to him, and, reaching upwards to her utmost stretch, hung herself fearlessly upon that arm which wields the destinies of the seventh part of the known world. He threw a look to our box, as if to say " I have found her;" and off they went together. In five minutes they passed again, and his Majesty made some effort to draw her to our box, but the little black sylph resisted, pulling in a contrary direction at his lofty shoulder with all her strength; on which he called out, "*Elle ne veut pas que je m'approche de vous; elle dit que je suis trop mauvaise société.*" Upon the second round, however, he succeeded in bringing his rebellious subject nearer; when, recognising his manœuvre, she plucked her arm away, gave him a smart slap on the wrist, and, saying "*Va t'en, je ne veux plus de toi,*" ran into the crowd. The Emperor, they assured me, was in an unusual good temper this evening.—I think there can be no doubt of it.

The Heritier now also took his station at our pillar. He inherits his father's majestic person and somewhat of the regularity of his face, but with the utter absence of the Emperor's unsympathising grandeur. On the contrary, the son has a face of much sentiment and feeling; the lips full,—the eyelids pensive— more of kindness than of character in his expression.

To him succeeded the Grand Duke Michael, wiping the heat from his forehead. A fine, bravo style of face, with somewhat ferocious moustaches,—a terrestrial likeness of the Emperor—earthly passions written on his high brow, but none of Jove's thunderbolts.

After this the Emperor's arm no longer

remained vacant, being occupied by a succession of masks, who by turns amused, flattered, or enlightened the Imperial ear. In like manner were his Highness the Prince Volkonski, Ministre de la Cour—Count Benkendorff, Chef de la Gendarmerie, de la Haute Police, et de la Police Secrète—Count Tchernitcheff, Ministre de la Guerre—and other high state and military officers, engaged; their attendance at masked balls being a part of their service.

This was my first introduction to such scenes: the second took place in the Salle de Noblesse, recently erected for public entertainments, and now considered the finest in Europe. The Salle itself is surrounded by a colonnade, twenty feet wide, of white marble pillars in couples supporting a gallery, ascended by a winding staircase at each corner. The vast arena for dancing is several feet lower than this colonnade, and entered thence by six different flights of noble steps. Of the exact dimensions I can give no measurement, save that seventy-five magnificent chandeliers were by no means crowded in position, or overpowering in light.

Attached to this grand apartment are other rooms fitted up with every luxury, and forming a circular suite, opening at each end into the colonnade I have described.

Here a repetition of the same half-glittering, half-sable scene was presented, but multiplied in number, for no less than two thousand seven hundred individuals, in and out of masks, were gathered together in the centre space, or circulating round the colonnade, or seated in the gallery aloft, or scattered through the suite of smaller rooms.

How in this wilderness of space and perplexity of crowd, where, under ordinary circumstances, a couple once separated had little chance of meeting again the same evening—how in this dazzling, shifting, confusing turmoil, among hundreds and thousands shrouded to the same form and colour—each solitary mask contrived to rejoin the party with whom she entered, was perhaps more a matter of anxiety to my mind than it was to theirs. The only way for these scattered particles to reunite is to fix upon some trysting-place—beneath the orchestra, or at the fourth pillar on the right hand, or on the sofa nearest the left, where, when tired with a solitary prowl after some object of her search, or weary with parading on the arm of some unknown individual,—who either proves impenetrably dull to her harmless sallies, or jumps to conclusions never intended, or indulges in innuendoes rather too plain of his own,—the weary mask may take refuge with some chance of finding a sister figure, who, led there by the same errand, immediately responds to her cautious watchword.

The only security on these occasions for your own enjoyment, or at any rate comfort, and for the entertainment which the assumption of this incognito promises to others, is to recognise the full advantages of your disguise—to forget your identity, and remember only your privileges—to bear in mind that when you assumed the mask you threw off all social responsibilities—to observe no ceremony—respect no person—to be flippant, contradictory, pert, and personal without fear of consequences—and in short to say little behind your mask that you would utter without it. As a pretty, witty, good-for-nothing little *intriguante* of the higher circles said to a timid novice on her first début in this disguise, "*Souvenez-vous en, ma chère, on n'a pas besoin d'un masque pour prêcher des sermons.*"

The general plan with the ladies of rank on these occasions is to acquire, by direct or indirect channels, some private information, some trivial anecdote of the every-day life or secret doings of the individual whom they intend, as the term is, to "*intriguer*"—to surprise him with the knowledge of some present he has made, or some letter he has sent, and which he considered unknown to all but the receiver—or to repeat verbatim some sentence which he supposes no one could have overheard; and by making the most of a little information to make him suppose them possessed of much more, and finally to heighten his perplexity by mystifying every avenue to their own identity.

For instance: Count ——— is the secret adorer of Madame ———, or fancies himself such. He gives her magnificent presents; and among the rest—the lady having pretty feet—he takes it into his head, with a lover's or a Russian's caprice, to surprise her with a foot-bath of the most delicate porcelain, which he orders at the celebrated *Magasin Anglais* in St. Petersburg. Well, at the next masked ball, a little brisk mask " *s'empare de son bras,*" and, after the first conventional impertinences of the place, she hangs her little black head sentimentally on one side, heaves a sigh, and exclaims, " *Ah! que Madame —— doit être heureuse! Que donnerais-je, moi, pour avoir un gentil petit bain de pied en porcelaine! J'ai aussi de jolis petits pieds, n'est-ce pas?*"—and with that she holds up a fairy foot, dressed in black shoe and stocking, with a coquettish gesture. "*Diable!*" thinks the Count: if she knows all about this foot-bath, of course she is also in the secret about the diamond bracelet, and the embroidered mantilla, and the Pensa shawl, and the letters I have written—"*qui sait?*" and, if the lady understand her *métier,* she probably contrives, by pursuing some right hit, or mystifying some wrong one, to elicit exactly that which he most intended to conceal; when, having spent all her store, or finding him in turn touching upon dangerous ground, she turns off with " *Mille remercimens pour tes informations. Tout le monde m'a dit que tu étais bête—à présent m'en voilà convaincue:*"—and these last words, pronounced in a louder tone, raise a laugh in the crowd around, who in this light, empty place, where sauciness is considered the only cleverness, and personality the best wit, are thankful for the smallest crumbs of amusement that may be thrown to them.

On this account it is that any lady's maid, or milliner's apprentice, or *couturière*, who, admitted with her basket of new dresses into the private boudoir of the highest ladies in the land, sees more behind the scenes than her superiors—is noticed for her pretty looks by *le mari*, or *l'ami*—hears familiarities of dialogue which her presence no ways restrains—and, if intent on this object, contrives to glean from the servants any further information she may want;—on this account it is that this class of persons, who frequently speak two or three languages correctly, and are not encumbered with that delicacy and timidity which restrains the really modest or the real gentlewoman, are generally most successful in perplexing the wits and piquing the curiosity of the gentlemen. At the Salle de Noblesse none who are not noble may find access; but in the latitudinarian nobility of Russia, and the transferability of a mask, this law is frequently evaded—and at the theatre these *grisettes* always play a conspicuous part.

The Emperor, when a mask has pleased his fancy, never rests till he has discovered her real name, and sets his secret police upon the scent with as much zest as after a political offender. The mask whom we had observed at the theatre on such familiar terms with him was recognised a few days after to be a little *modiste* from the most fashionable milliner's in Petersburg, whose frequent errands to the Empress had furnished her with a few graphic touches of the Imperial character.

But to return to the ladies of the highest

society who make use of this disguise for mere purposes of raillery and good-natured mischief. This is the best aspect under which the levity of a masked ball can be considered, and to enact this with success or impunity requires an intimate knowledge of society, a perfect mastery of the current languages, and, not least, a tolerable practice in the humours of a masquerade. Even without the first qualification, however, a mask may have some chance of success, for *l'esprit d'intrigue* inherent more or less in every woman, and *l'esprit de vanité* inherent more or less in every man, contrive to give both means and subject for that saucy banter which is the groundwork of a mask's popularity.

But this, I repeat, is the best aspect of these Russian masked balls. I leave it to the astuteness of others to conclude the uses and abuses which must ensue from this temporary and utter freedom in a sex whose chief charm consists in seeking and needing protection. More especially in a country where society is placed under the utmost external restraint—where even the common courtesies of good breeding are viewed with suspicious eyes,—where a young man can hardly converse with a young woman without laying her open to censure, and a woman is not free to indulge her love of admiration, or a man to approach her with the same, till such time as both the one and the other ought to cease, viz., till she is married. I do not exaggerate when I say that two-thirds of the masks in this Liberty Hall were married women, whose husbands knew not or cared not whether they were there.

At the same time, in a country where unfortunately neither promotion, nor justice, nor redress, generally speaking, are to be had without interest, this means of directly reaching the Imperial ear, or that of the chief officers of the state—of presenting a living anonymous letter—of dropping information which they are bound, if not to favour, at all events not to take amiss—is immensely resorted to. The Emperor has been known to remonstrate loudly at being annoyed with business or complaint in these few hours of relaxation; but this is rather to be attributed to the awkwardness or embarrassment of the poor petitioner, who, feeling the welfare of a father or brother, or of a whole family, hanging upon the force of her slender words,—addressing for the first time the awful individual whose word makes and unmakes a law,—and ashamed perhaps of the disguise to which she has been compelled, can neither command the calmness nor adroitness necessary to smooth the way for her blunter petition.

On the other hand, where the complainant, by a happy address or a well-timed flattery, has disposed the Imperial palate for the reception of more sober truths, her case has been listened to with humanity, and met by redress. More than once the Emperor was observed engaged with a mask in conversation which had evidently digressed from levity into a more serious strain, and was overheard to thank the mask for her information and promise the subject his attention.

In consequence of the taste which his Majesty has of late years evinced for this species of amusement, the masked balls have greatly increased in number and resort. Previous to being incapacitated by bad health the Empress also equally partook of them, and it is said greatly enjoyed being addressed with the same familiarity as any of her subjects. Her Majesty has even been the cause of severe terrors to many an unfortunate individual, who, new to the scene, or not recognising by filial instinct the maternal arm which pressed his, has either himself indulged in too much licence of speech, or given the Imperial mask to understand that he found hers devoid of interest.

But let us quit these scenes—at best, a masquerade is a *bad* place.

LETTER THE TWENTY-THIRD.

Chief houses of reception in St. Petersburg—Freedom of the Imperial family—Restraint of the subject—Absence of etiquette—Ball at Prince Y.'s—Ball at Countess L.'s—Beauties of the high circles—Ball at Madame L.'s—General aspect of manners and morals—Dress—Servants—The Grand Duchess Helen.

AFTER this lengthened comment upon the high Russian society as seen beneath the black cloud of a mask, it now follows to describe its usual face stripped of all disguise, save that which every individual assumes more or less on quitting his own circle. At this time all the noble and wealthy houses in Petersburg are vying with one another in the number and splendour of their entertainments—endeavouring to compress as much pleasure as possible into the few remaining weeks before Lent, when balls, theatres, and masquerades are denied them, and their only passetems reduced to soirées, concerts, and tableaux.

The principal families whose wealth enables them to maintain this rate of expenditure in this most expensive of all capitals are those of Prince Youssoupoff, Count Cheremeteff, Count Woronzoff Daschkoff, Count Strogonoff, Count Laval, Countess Razumoffski, General Sukasannet, M. Lazareff, &c., &c., whose entertainments are conducted on a scale of luxury, which, in this extreme, it is confined to a Russian capital to display. The passion for entertainment and show is inherent in a Russian breast. However husband and wife may differ on other points, they are sure to agree in a feeling which is mingled of equal parts —hospitality and vanity. Entertainments, equipages, *toilette*,—whatever appertans to show, is here found in perfection; and if you look from the window at the peasant-woman trudging past in her red and yellow, or catch sight of the gilded spire or cupola towering above the snow roofs, all tells of the same predominant disposition.

The Emperor, who, as Grand Duke Nicholas, was noted for the simplicity of his tastes, and could hardly be induced to enter a place of amusement, now resorts to them with an increasing pleasure from which some augur no auspicious result;—frequents the houses of his nobility and generals, who would spend to their last kopeck, and often go beyond it, to entertain him suitably—while the Empress's love of amusement and dress, besides inoculating her august spouse, has fixed a standard for merit, and exacted a rate of expenditure, which, to say the least, was not required to stimulate the already too-expensively disposed Russian.

For instance: a splendid *déjeûner*, which is to turn winter into summer, and Russia into Arcadia, is arranged to be given by one of the first families in St. Petersburg. One of the generals in closest attendance upon the Emperor's person is commissioned to intercede for the honour of His Majesty's presence, and obtains a gracious assent. When the day comes, however, and money is wanted, Baron Stieglitz, the great banker, shows how far the wrong page of the account-book has been encroached upon, and refuses the necessary advances. What is to be done? Money must be had.— You can't put off a monarch till a more convenient season (though we, thoughtless mortals, will put off a weightier monarch than he)— you can't "tie up your knocker, say you are sick, you are dead,"—when the Emperor and Empress of all the Russias are expected. The necessary sum—and in a country where Nature gives nothing, the expense of such an entertainment is enormous—is therefore borrowed in haste, and at a usurious interest— for fifty per cent. is demanded and accepted on such exigencies—while all thoughts of future inconvenience are drowned in the flattering honours of the day: "*L'Empereur était très content,*" or "*L'Impératrice a beaucoup dansé,*" is sufficient atonement.

But if you examine a little closer, and ask a few troublesome questions, it will be found that even this dearly-purchased honour is not productive of the pleasure that might be supposed. Wherever the Imperial family appear, however great their affability, however sincere and obvious their desire to please and be pleased, the mere fact of their presence throws a restraint, a *gêne* over the whole assembly, who are depressed rather than exhilarated by the cold gaze of the Imperial eye, and who feel that the whole attention of their hosts is concentred on one object.

The young military are in apprehension lest their uniform should not be found in strict accordance, to the shape of a button or the length of a spur, with the latest regulation;— the young ladies, and equally their chaperons, are in anxiety lest any awkwardness of dress or manner should incur the censure, however pleasantly expressed, of her to whom all adjudge the purest taste in *toilette* and *tournure;*— while the host and hostess suffer real fear lest any unbecoming speech or incident should transpire to render the recollection of their hospitalities obnoxious to their illustrious guests.

The anxiety attendant on the reception of any monarch by his subject must at all times be proportioned to the honour, but here the total absence of all etiquette multiplies the difficulty an hundred-fold. For it must be remembered that the more limited the monarch, the more absolute the etiquette—and *vice versâ*. In Russia, therefore, where the Zar is "*la loi vivante*"—the constitution in person—no etiquette can exist, or rather only such as he pleases for the time being. Whatever he does is right—he cannot demean himself. His actions are restrained by no law of ceremony,—by no obligation of dignity,—by no fear of public opinion. His rank takes care of itself—it wants no propping—it is in one piece, like his own Alexander's column. His only restraint is his own responsibility, and in no country is this so awful. He and his consort, according to their pleasure or disposition, can either render moderation habitual, or extravagance meritorious—morality fashionable, or frivolity praiseworthy. They can qualify vices to foibles, or ennoble vanities to virtues. The example of the Crown is as imperative in private life, as its will in public life, and nowhere is it more greedily imitated.

But to return to etiquette. However tedious and troublesome its formalities, they are not half so onerous to a host as his perpetual anxiety and real responsibility in a court where there is no rule for manners except the caprice of the monarch or the tact of the subject.

The truth of these remarks was exemplified at a ball at Prince Y.'s, which his Imperial Majesty honoured with his presence, and where, though he was obviously as condescending as his hosts were zealous, yet that stately figure in the portal, presiding in unbending beauty like a being from another world, weighed down the hilarity of all present.

The hotel of Prince Y., situated upon the Moika Canal, is one of the many splendid mansions in St. Petersburg. The grand suite of apartments is adorned with a collection of pictures by the old masters, some few of which are of signal merit, especially two exquisite Claudes, a Parmegiano, and a Sasso Ferrato.

In the *Salle des Antiquités* were also some valuable objects of art, particularly an antique foot, while statues by Canova and other modern sculptors, with groups in ivory and alabaster, and collections of costly china and silver ornaments, &c., were dispersed about the rooms. Also two portfolios beneath glass cases, containing original letters from Peter the Great and Catherine II. to some "*Excellence*" of this princely house.

The ball at Countess L.'s was more spirited, for here the Heritier, accompanied by his brother-in-law, the Duke de Leuchtenberg, was the sole representative of the Imperial family, and, joining in the dance, his fine person and gentle demeanour only lent an additional grace to the scene.

Here, from the absence of restraint, I had more opportunity of noting the female beauty of St. Petersburg, among whom were foremost the Princess Belozelsky Belozersky, a lovely specimen of a "*Petite Russe*," with *nez retroussé*, large languishing black eyes, hair bending from the root in the most graceful volutes, beautiful teeth, and fair skin, with a *petite taille* of the utmost delicacy;—Countess Woronzoff Daschkoff, an *espiègle* gipsy, whose *polissonnerie* of expression and speech has attracted her a species of popularity in this capital which a more regular or a more cautious beauty would not attain;—Princess Narischkin, with skin of ivory and eyes of jet;—Madame Zavadoffsky, whose plenitude of beauty the English world has seen;—the Princess Marie Bariatinsky, a fine intellectual face, with a somewhat English calm of expression, and such magnificent *chevelure* as seems to betoken strength of mind as well as of person;—Madame Stoluipin, late Princess Troubetzkoi, a graceful *nouvelle mariée;*—Mademoiselle Karamsin, the pretty maid of honour;—and last, though never least in the garden of beauty, the lovely Annette—who, with a new tiara of diamonds on her head, and a single emerald, a unique stone, large as an old-fashioned miniature or a teacup reversed, and surrounded by a single row of *solitaire* diamonds, blazing like Hermione's carbuncle on her chest, and her " *belles épaules Grecques,*" as the Empress has aptly termed them, bared to view, looked, what few do, as much to advantage in the dazzling and heated ball-room as among the cool orange-groves of her own Fall.

The *toilettes* and display of jewels were beyond all description gorgeous, and the graceful though slender set which adorned the person of the pretty English Ambassadress were pronounced to be " *assez joli.*"

This house, situated on the English Quay, is also magnificent: hall, staircase, and apartments of the utmost beauty of form and luxury of arrangement. Here was likewise a collection of pictures, fewer in number, but more select in value, than those at Prince Y.'s— a Fra Bartolomeo very conspicuous: also a small antique room with sculptures from Pompeii, and mosaic pavement from the baths of Tiberius in the isle of Capri. But hidden glories were yet behind, for our hostess, who has the repute of being " *un peu bizarre,*" not thinking it worth her while to display all the resources of her mansion for the Heir of all the

Russias, had refrained from lighting up her grandest reception-rooms till such time as the Emperor himself should be present. It seemed strange, in the midst of all this splendour, in which royalty mixed with so much condescension, to reflect that our hostess had a son-in-law and daughter exiled for life to Siberia for participation in the rebellion of 1826, and that she herself had not escaped either blame or punishment on that occasion, though of her present restoration to Imperial favour there can be no question.

The entertainments, however, which have been most successful this season, are the weekly balls of M. de L., the rich Armenian, whose lady, a Circassian by birth, and most decidedly so in physiognomy, presides with much grace. For these balls no regular invitations are circulated, the fashion having emanated from the court of giving the most costly fêtes in a kind of impromptu manner. Madame L. is merely understood to receive on Thursdays, and her crowding guests find all the *apprêts* of the most splendid ball. The Imperial family, if the expression may be allowed, had not been admitted to these soirées, but, in consequence of a condescending observation from his Imperial Highness the Grand Duke Michael, "*Tout le monde parle de vos jolis bals, Madame L.: pourquoi ne m'invitez-vous pas?*" the next Thursday was distinguished by his presence.

But wherever the Grand Duke appears, he takes the strict disciplinarian with him. Before his Imperial Highness had been in the ball-room half an hour he knit his brows with an ominous expression, and, striding up to a young officer who had just halted from the waltz, and was dreaming at that moment of no other eyes in the world but his lady's, the Grand Duke startled him with the uncomfortable words, "*Vasche Sporne schlischkom glinie*"—your spurs are too long—"*Aux arrêts:*" and sent him without further parley from his partner's arms to the guardhouse. The Imperial frown and action, and the young man's discomfited retreat, were seen by many, and the incident was soon buzzed in whispers round the room, greatly to the anxiety and annoyance of host and hostess.

Such balls as these I have described, however brilliant and dazzling in relation, are not otherwise than very dull in reality; for here, as in France, society is so perversely constituted that no enjoyment is to be reaped save by infringing its rules. A "*jeune personne*,"—in other words, an unmarried woman—is considered a mere cipher in society, danced with seldom, conversed with seldomer, and under these circumstances looks forward to her *mariage de convenance* as the period which, as I have said before, is to commence that which it ought to close. From the day of her marriage she is free—responsible to no one, so that she overstep not the rules of convention, for the liberty of her conduct; while her husband is rather piqued than otherwise if her personal charms fail to procure her the particular attentions of his own sex. "*Personne ne lui fait la cour*" is the most disparaging thing that can be said of a young wife. It is sad to see the difference in a short season from the retiring girl to one whose expression and manners seem to say that "Honesty coupled to beauty is to have honey sauce to sugar." Nor is it easy for an inexperienced young woman, gifted with domestic tastes, or marrying from affection, to stem the torrent of ridicule of those who would pull others down to justify themselves.

This social evil is seen in the more glaring colours from the total absence of all rational tastes or literary topics. In other countries it is lamented, and with justice, that literature and education should be made the things of fashion—how infinitely worse is it when they are condemned by the same law! In other countries all fashion, as such, is condemned as bad—how infinitely worse is it where the bad is the fashion! Here it is absolute *mauvais genre* to discuss a rational subject — mere *pédanterie* to be caught upon any topics beyond dressing, dancing, and a "*jolie tournure*." The superficial accomplishments are so superficialised as scarcely to be considered to exist—Russia has no literature, or rather none to attract a frivolous woman;—and political subjects, with all the incidental chit-chat which the observances, anniversaries, &c., of a constitutional government bring more or less into every private family, it is needless to observe, exist not. What then remains? Sad to say, nothing, absolutely nothing, for old and young, man and woman, save the description, discussion, appreciation, or depreciation of *toilette*—varied by a little *cuisine* and the witless wit called *l'esprit du salon*. To own an indifference or an ignorance on the subject of dress, further than a conventional and feminine compliance, would be wilfully to ruin your character equally with the gentlemen as with the ladies of the society; for the former, from some inconceivable motive, will discuss a new bracelet or a new dress with as much relish as if they had hopes of wearing it, and with as great a precision of technical terms as if they had served at a *marchand de modes*. It may seem almost incredible, but here these externals so entirely occupy every thought, that the highest personage in the land, with the highest in authority under him, will meet and discuss a lady's *coiffure,* or even a lady's *corset,* with a gusto and science as incomprehensible in them, to say the least, as the emulation of coachman slang in some of our own eccentric nobility. Whether, in a state where individuals are judged by every idle word, or rather where every idle word is literally productive of mischief, the blandishments of the toilet, from their political innocuousness, are considered safest ground for the detention of mischievous spirits, I must leave undecided; but very certain it is that in the high circles of Petersburg it would seem, from the prevailing tone of conversation, that nothing was considered more meritorious than a pretty face and figure, or more interesting than the question how to dress it.

Added to this wearying theme, it is the bad taste of the day to indulge in an indelicacy of language which some aver to proceed from the example of the court of Prussia, and which renders at times even the trumperies of toilet or jewellery rather a grateful change of subject.

Let it not be imagined, however, that no individuals with intellectual tastes or cultivated minds are to be found in these circles. On the contrary, it is an additional proof of the excellence of these gifts that, in an atmosphere where they may be said to be equally persecuted and starved, there are many who cultivate them as sedulously as they conceal them. It is not from lack of education that the frivolity of the Russian women is derived, for their tuition is generally conducted with great care by those placed as preceptresses over them; but such is the withering spell of fashion, that a young woman entering society is as anxious to hide the acquirements as any other *gaucheries* of the school-room, and it must be said generally succeeds.

Languages, which they imbibe in childhood, are the only demonstrations of acquirement permitted. English is heard on all sides, though it is little gratifying to hear our sober tongue applied to ideas by no means corresponding.

According to the statement of some elders of the society, things were very different beneath the studious reign of Catherine II., and the dignified benevolence of the late Empress Mother. Now, however, the habit of frivolity is so strong that, by the rising generation especially, any deviation from the established topics is met with so real and innocent a mirth as almost to make one forgive its misapplication. How many graceful beings are there in the circles I am describing "born for better things," and whom one longs to remove from a pernicious atmosphere! By nature the Russian woman of rank is a most charming and winning creature—uniting both the witchery and the heroism of a Frenchwoman, and the seductiveness of an Asiatic, with an inherent grace and polish exclusively her own. How the same woman can drill her noble heart and high spirit down to the palling ennui of a frivolity unrelieved by the semblance of animation, and scarcely of mischief —to the mill-round of a senseless luxury, without comfort for its vindication or art for its plea—is an enigma only to be solved in the Proteus-nature of human perversity. But the Russian woman ought only to be seen in other lands: there she feels herself emancipated; and there, proverbially, she is one of the sweetest types of womankind.

Speaking of dress, it must be remembered that this all paramount item in St. Petersburg is one purchased at greater expense than in any other fashionable capital. The Russian manufactories are utterly eschewed by all of any pretensions in society, and foreign goods pay an amount of duty which doubles their price. The very climate induces, nay exacts, expenses which in other countries are optional. A *demi-saison* toilette, that *entremets* on fashion's board with which many dispense, is here absolutely necessary. In short, there are endless necessary gradations between the winter's coat of mail and the summer's cobweb. Even in the livery of the servants these extremes of heat and cold induce expenses not known elsewhere.

The number of men-servants in every room is a most striking feature. Here they lounge the day long, and are ready to obey the call from the suite within, for very few houses are furnished with bells, and even in these cases the habit of calling is rather too strong to be omitted. One potent reason for the swarms of men-servants is, that a Russian establishment acknowledges not that useful member called a *housemaid*—between the lady's-maid and the man-servant there is no intermediate link. These latter are all serfs, either the master's own, or those of another landed proprietor, to whom they frequently pay more than half their wages for the freedom of serving in this capacity. Generally speaking, however, they are a happy, good-humoured, attached race, who wait upon a lady, and especially a young and a pretty one, with a chivalrous kind of devotion. The actual and immense distance between the two classes permits of much seeming familiarity, on the same principle as the absoluteness of the monarchy extinguishes all etiquette. A young lady will call her man-servant 'brat' or brother; and he will speak of and to her as *Jelisavetta Ivanovna*, or Elizabeth the daughter of John. If you drive to call on a married sister, you tell the attendant not "to the Princess ———," but "*k'Marie Alexandrovna*,"—to Marie daughter of Alexander. This custom is universal. The sons and daughters of the Imperial house are spoken of in the same manner. *Michael Pavlovitch* distinguishes the Grand Duke Michael from *Michael Nicolaievitch*, the little Grand Duke, son of the Emperor. The Empress is always designated as *Alexandra Feodorovna*, and the Grand Duchess Helen as *Helena Pavlovna*.

This last-named illustrious lady, consort of the Grand Duke Michael, and by birth a Princess of Wirtemberg, has more particularly suffered from this present condemnation of all rational tastes. Endued by nature with a most studious and reflective mind, and educated with corresponding advantages, her Imperial Highness was thrown alone, at a very early age, into a court where such qualities, far from finding encouragement, hardly met with sufferance. Not her great personal beauty nor acknowledged charm of manner could redeem the unpopular circumstance of her heterodox tastes.

Of her it may be said, "*qui de son age n'a pas l'esprit, de son age a tous les malheurs,*" for this inadaptation between the properties of her mind and the soil in which they were placed has exposed her Imperial Highness to trials, the peculiar painfulness of which may be better imagined than described.

From a combination of circumstances, the honour of admission to the presence of the Grand Duchess Helen was on several occasions allowed me. Owing to the delicacy of her health, as well as to her preference for retirement, she had not appeared in public during the season. My first view of this lady was therefore in her own beautiful apartments in the *Palais Michel*. Her Imperial Highness is about two-and-thirty years of age, with a tall graceful person and great beauty of feature and complexion. Her three daughters were frequently with her. Their education, which has come under the Grand Duchess's immediate superintendence, has been conducted on a directly opposite system to that usually observed in the high circles of Petersburg, and has been successful in producing, or rather in retaining, those natural and bashful graces which are the best inheritance of youth. This was quite refreshing to witness after the artificial and premature ease,—the early and unbecoming self-possession of the children of the nobility, who, introduced from their tenderest years into the circles of society, lose much more than they gain by exchanging the charms of childhood for those of a more advanced age.

The beauties, political and picturesque, of England, and the kindness she had there experienced, seemed favourite recollections with her Imperial Highness, while the condescension of her manners, the polished intelligence of her conversation, and the inexpressible interest attached to her person and history, have excited those in me which will never subside. May the future be rich in blessings to Helena Pavlovna!

The Palais Michel is one of the grandest edifices in Petersburg;—the entrance-hall and grand staircase are celebrated for their splendour and extent. The birth of the Grand Duke Michael having taken place after the accession of the Emperor Paul, he inherited greater private property than any of his brothers.

The death of the Emperor Paul is a subject now discussed without any great reserve. Owing to his tyrannical, or, it may better be said, insane excesses, beneath which no individual in the empire could be considered safe, it was agreed upon for the public safety, and with the connivance of his eldest son, the late Alexander, to depose him from the government and imprison him for life. His immense personal strength frustrated, however, all possibility of capture, while his recognition of the assailants rendered his murder necessary. Count Pahlen was the individual who strangled him with his pocket-handkerchief, and bore ever after the sobriquet of *Schnupftuch Pahlen*. If any one to this day ask, "Who was the Countess T. by birth?" the answer, as a matter of course, is, "The only child of *Schnupftuch Pahlen.*"

It is said that Alexander never shook off the sense of indirect participation in his father's murder, by which also all punishment of the perpetrators was interdicted to him. They were merely sent out of Russia to travel.

LETTER THE TWENTY-FOURTH.

Prince Pierre Volkonski—Count Benkendorff—Count Nesselrode—Taglioni—The Empress—Madame Allan—The Russian theatre—The first Russian opera—Characteristics of the three classes of society in Russia—Power of the monarch—Railroad to Zarskoe Selo—The Great Palace—Reminiscences of the Emperor Alexander—The Emperor's Palace—The Arsenal—General impressions.

AND now, having inspected the fair ranks of beauty in this capital, it may be allowable to pass on to battalions of a hardier nature and older growth, whose martial figures and glittering apparel greatly enhance the picturesque effect of every saloon. Indeed, such is the predominance of the military, that on entering society all the male guests, at first glance, appear to be enthralled in uniform, and only on nearer inspection are the black shades of a few civilians seen gliding amongst them. In both classes—though as often as not civil and military offices of equal importance are combined beneath the same gorgeous uniform—it is highly interesting to observe individuals whose names are interwoven with the history of Russian camps or Russian politics, and whom the mind has already invested with the halo of the past. Foremost in rank in the society of Petersburg stands the Prince Pierre Volkonski, *Grand Ministre de la Cour*, distinguished outwardly by his diamond insignia of office, and by a medal of the Winter Palace, set in magnificent diamonds, presented to him on the rebuilding of this edifice, both of which hang gleaming with his other decorations on the left side of the ample breast of his uniform. This prince has the direction of all the expenditure of the Imperial family—the office of arranging all entertainments and festivities: the immediate protection of the Empress's person also devolves on him, he being her official attendant at all public places and on all occasions of travel. It is he who has the charge of the crown jewels, and the care of providing the necessary sets of jewels for the daughters of the Emperor as they attain womanhood. It was amusing to hear the good prince, who has a manly exterior and truly martial air, sigh over the expenses of the Grand Duchess Marie's late marriage—for by the Emperor's will she retains her maiden title—and calculate what would be necessary for "Olga," and what "*pour la femme de l'Héritier.*" From the check which the prudence and responsibility of Prince Pierre Volkonski sometimes place over the lavish expenditure of the court, and from his unceasing efforts to detect imposition and lessen extravagance, this nobleman, like many another in the same situation, has attracted much undeserved ill will to his person.

Count Benkendorff is another most conspicuous character both in Russian history and in the Petersburg world. This nobleman may be cited as a rare instance of one who, while he is the intimate friend and confidant, in short, what may be termed the favourite, of the Emperor, is himself the most popular man with all classes of his subjects; and thus the connection, both official and amical, which, ever since the period of the accession, has existed between the reigning sovereign and himself, is one equally honourable to both. By the union of the happiest tact, the profoundest discretion, and the soundest integrity, Count Benkendorff has obtained an influence with his Majesty which, exerted only on the side of humanity and benevolence, is hailed with pleasure by every one. In his more especial department as head of the secret police he has earned for himself a confidence and affection which certainly no *chef* in this ominous capacity ever enjoyed before, and it is matter of universal gratulation throughout the empire that this office is placed in such hands.

Count Benkendorff is brother to the late popular ambassadress to London, the Princess Lieven.

Count Nesselrode is another distinguished individual of private popularity and public celebrity, who enlivens these circles with his astute sense and playful wit.

And many other great names might be specified if space allowed.

It seems natural that individuals with whom politics necessarily occupy so large a portion of time and thought, who return direct from the senate, or from the private conference, to their domestic circles, should involuntarily continue the train of idea aloud. But such is the necessity or the habit of discretion, that not a word transpires to betray the occupation or the circle they have just quitted; save perhaps to a wife or daughter—" *L'Empereur t'a trouvée bien jolie hier au bal,*" or " *t'a mise délicieuse.*"

Once, on occasion of a small dinner where Prince Volkonski, Count Benkendorff, the venerable Prince Lubetski, and other distinguished characters, were united, the conversation fell upon the organisation of the senate—the difficulty of expressing themselves in Russian, now the language of the state—the little practice which the nature of the government affords for addressing numbers;—but of the matter there discussed, *Gott behüte!* not one word.

From the national enjoyment which Russians of all classes take in every species of scenic diversion, the theatre is particularly a popular amusement. Taglioni is now the great star of attraction; and, *caressée* by the Imperial family, worshipped by the young nobles, applauded by overflowing audiences, and most munificently paid, this poetess of the ballet has every reason to be satisfied with her northern visit. But poor Taglioni has suffered deeply here; and, while she dances at night under the least possible encumbrance of gauze drapery, appears by day, her little girl in her hand, shrouded in the deepest widow's mourning— not for her husband, but for a lover, who it seems had proved the more constant friend of the two. At all events, there are not many in Petersburg who may throw stones;—nor, to do them justice, do they seem disposed.

Herself at the *Grand Théâtre*, Madame Allan at the *Théâtre Michel*, draw alternate crowds. Taglioni's most popular character is the *Tyen*, or *l'Ombre*, in which she has danced sixty times in succession. Here she is introduced on the stage only to die in the first act by the jealous hand of a rival, and to re-appear during the rest as a mere airy spirit, in which capacity her ethereal movements and floating sylphlike graces, for which an earthly form seems too gross, have full play. Every winged bound, or languid glide, or clean-cut pirouette, was hailed with deafening applause; the Emperor and his heir clapping their hands with all their might, and the vast parterre of military vociferating her name, which, beneath the liquid open intonation of a Russian throat, was metamorphosed to a sound which must have struck as strangely upon her ear as upon my own.

The decorative scenes of the great theatre are particularly magnificent. In the ballet of the *Tyen,* by a novel and most happy arrangement, the entire background of the stage was filled with an unbroken sheet of mirror, before which various figures moved in graceful cadence—or rather what appeared to be such—for the whole was an ocular deception brought about by an ingenious disposition of the figures, each of whom being accompanied and strictly mimicked in action by a figure of exactly similar size and costume, with a sheet of transparent gauze intervening, all the effect of reflection was produced. It occurred to few that the audience found no reflection in this apparent mirror.

It was here that the only opportunity of seeing the Empress occurred—her Majesty's state of health forbidding her all other participation in the amusements of the season. And even here, in order to avoid the risk of exposure to the air, her Majesty arrived in her morning dress, being preceded by her waiting-women with several *cartons* which were visible in the withdrawing-room behind the Imperial box, and where her Majesty attired herself for the evening. The theatres are all heated, and sometimes to an excessive degree—the thermometer in our box standing at 82°. Her Majesty's malady appeared to be of a highly nervous nature, with an incessant restlessness of person and change of position. Her Majesty's person bore traces of symmetry, but in her present debilitated and emaciated state it was impossible to judge of her former personal attractions.

The Imperial family generally occupy a box

next to the stage and contiguous to *la loge Michel:* opposite is a corresponding and similarly decorated box set apart for *le Ministre de la Cour.* The centre state-box is seldom resorted to, and was more frequently occupied by the Queen of one of the lately conquered Asiatic tribes, who resides in Petersburg upon a pension from the Crown—one whom a lively companion designated as " *la vieille fée Carabosse,*" and who truly, in a fantastic Oriental costume, and attended by ladies of the same style of physiognomy, appeared to preside over a very court of ugliness.

In addition to his other numerous charges, the censorship of the theatres falls to the share of Count Benkendorff, who scrutinizes every play before its performance. Nevertheless the French theatre is not so select as to render that long habitude necessary to follow every word of a rapid French dialogue by any means desirable.

Occasionally Taglioni's ballet gave place to a very different scene, both as respects actors and audience—namely, to the performance of a Russian opera, the first ever written, called

"*Jishn za Zara*," or "Your Life for your Zar:" the music by Glinki, the words by Baron Rosen. This opera, equally from the popularity of the subject and the beauty and nationality of the music, has met with the utmost success. The plot of the piece, as far as we could fathom it, was the concealment and subsequent discovery of the true Zar, and his final coronation at Moscow, with a splendid representation of the Kremlin. This is woven up with a love-tale, and rendered interesting by the fidelity of a fine old Russian with a long beard and a bass voice, who eventually pays for his adherence with his life.

The music was strikingly national, and one trio in particular appeared to combine every peculiar beauty of Russian melody and pathos, and will doubtless acquire a European celebrity. It was very strange to see true Russians personating true Russians—gallery, pit, and stage being equally filled with the same bearded and caftaned figures. The national feeling seemed in every heart and on every lip; any allusion to the Zar—and the subject was thickly strewn with them—was pronounced by the actors with the utmost animation, and responded to by electric shouts from the audience. Nor was there any casual inducement for this display of loyalty, for neither his Majesty nor any of the Imperial family were present.

These are the scenes, more than any luxurious entertainment or military parade, which reveal the strength of the Crown.

From careful observation, and the judgment of those longer experienced, it would appear that the guarantees for the continued stability of Russia lie exclusively in the person of the monarch and in the body of the people. In the nobility, whose elements of national character fall far beneath those of his serf, the monarch finds no efficient help. Foreign education and contact has, with a few brilliant exceptions, rendered them adepts in the luxury and frivolity rather than in the humanity of civilization, or grafted them with democratic Utopian ideas that in no state, and least of all in Russia, can bring forth good fruit. The Emperor, therefore, has full ground for the double mistrust with which he views money taken out of the empire and pernicious ideas brought in.

Again, in the so-called middle class—here the mere excrescence of a partial civilization, who have renounced all of their nationality save its barbarity—all real support to the Crown seems still further removed. These occupy the lower departments of the state, clogging all straightforward dealing, perverting the real intention of the laws, and intercepting every humane Imperial act by the most cunning and unprincipled dishonesty. What will be said of other and more important intentions of the Emperor when it is known that the snuffbox destined to reward some act of benevolence, which leaves the Imperial hands embossed with diamonds, reaches those of its destined owner deprived of every stone! And no redress is to be had under laws where an equal accumulation of formalities and liability to abuse meet the innocent at every turn.

Despised by the nobles, this class retaliate by a species of persecution which it is impossible to guard against. No lion's mouth, or familiars of the Inquisition, are needed in a state of things where, ere a false denunciation can be sifted and dismissed, the denounced is equally ruined in purse and worn out with constant care; and nowhere, sad to say, are denunciations of this kind so frequent as at this time in Russia—nowhere so tedious and ruinous in their exposure. Rank, consideration, long service, and high reputation are of no avail. Once an accusation is laid, however it may bear the stamp of malice, it must distil through all the corkscrew windings of the Russian law, ere the property of the accused be released from sequestration, or his mind from the most corroding anxiety—and this done, there is neither compensation for the injured nor punishment for the injurer, who has thus cloaked his cupidity or revenge under the semblance of what the people honour most, *viz.* his loyalty.

This class it is who have made the Russian courts of justice a byword and a proverb—who have called down upon Russia the unmerited sarcasm of being "*pourrie avant d'être mure*"—while, by a natural retribution, the name of

Chinovnik, or the betitled (for these men are generally distinguished by an order), is fast becoming the synonym for low dishonesty and intrigue. The national proverb which says no Russian without "*Chai, Tschi, and Chin*"—tea, sour-krout, and a title—is perfectly true; but the sarcasm on the latter is derived from the abuse of a noble principle. Peter the Great, the well-intentioned founder of this rage for orders in Russia, was right when he foresaw the veneration with which the mass of the people would regard every individual invested with an insignia emanating direct from the sovereign, and calculated thereby on putting a wholesome power into the hands of the middle ranks: but he reckoned too soon on the formation of this class, which, to be safe or to be useful, must be gradual and spontaneous in growth; and the careless and lavish hand with which orders have been distributed since his reign has only debased the distinction without elevating the possessor.

It is predicted that, should any political convulsion occur in Russia, this miserable class, who suffer the double ill fate of ideas below their station, and a station above their maintenance, would meet with the nobility in jarring collision, and with equal danger to both, while the Crown, firmly seated in the instinctive loyalty of the people, would have nought to fear. By a providential adaptation which surpasses all speculation of legislative philosophy, the people of Russia venerate their sovereign simply because he is absolute. With them respect for the anointed sovereign is a religion; and to restrict him by human ordinances would be to strip him of his divine credentials. What Zar has yet been dethroned or murdered by an act of the people?

What a magnificent engine, thus weighted, is the power of a Russian sovereign! With the mind filled by the absoluteness of his sway, and the eye possessed by the magnificence of his person, Nicholas I. seems too grand a combination for mortal ken. But these are subjects beyond my intention. Let me now resume my outward life.

A day has been devoted to Zarskoe Selo—

literally Imperial village, to which a railroad from Petersburg offers the easiest access. It was a sharp frost with a beautiful sun, the steam pouring off against a hard bright sky. The moment of starting being delayed, we quitted the carriage to hasten to the stationhouse. Here was congregated together that picturesque crowd which the variety of Russian costumes always offer:—officers in grey military cloaks—women with every bright colour on their persons—priests in Rembrandt colour and costume—Mougiks with aquiline noses and long beards, and even a Russian specimen of Pickwick! We placed ourselves in the fourth carriage, commodiously fitted up with soft easy seats, and, pulling down the glass, braved the frost for a short time to contemplate the peculiarity of the landscape.

Russia is the country for railroads—no hills, no vales—no beautiful parks to intersect—no old family hearts to break. On either hand was a plain of snow, so devoid of object as hardly to indicate the swiftness of our movements. Above half-way appeared in the distance a castellated mansion, where Catherine II. was wont to relax from the Empress; and upon the horizon was the slight but only elevation of Zarskoe Selo. The distance, about twenty-five wersts, we accomplished in twenty minutes.

Alighting, we took to an open sledge, and drove to the great palace, which presents a long and dull front decorated with figures and pilasters, formerly covered with gilding, now replaced by yellow paint. This palace has, since Alexander's death, been abandoned by the Imperial family, and is therefore bare of furniture, though with great richness of walls and floors; the former either in simple white and gold, or hung with rich silks—the latter parqueted in the most graceful designs and tender colours, still as fresh as when first laid down. The two apartments of most attraction were the lapis-lazuli room, where strips of this stone are inlaid into the walls, with a few slabs and tables of the same; and the amber room, where the walls are literally panelled with this material in various architectural shapes; the arms of Frederic the Great, by whom it was presented to Catherine II., being moulded in different compartments, with the Imperial cipher, the Russian E., for Ekaterina. Two grand ball-rooms were also conspicuous, the upper end of each being occupied by a collection of the most splendid china vases placed on circular tiers up to the ceiling, and designated by the same Imperial E.

The whole palace respired recollections of Catherine II. There were her private rooms, with the small door communicating with the reigning favourite's apartments; and the gentle descent leading into the garden by which she was wheeled up and down when infirmity had deprived her of the use of her limbs.

But the sentiment of the edifice dwelt in the simple rooms of the late Emperor Alexander, whom all remember with affection, and speak of with melancholy enthusiasm. His apartments have been kept exactly as he left them when he departed for Taganrog. His writing-cabinet, a small light room with scagliola walls, seemed as if the Imperial inmate had just turned his back. There was his writing-table in confusion—his well-blotted case—the pens black with ink. Through this was his simple bed-room, where in an alcove, on a slight camp bedstead with linen coverlet, lay the fine person and troubled heart of poor Alexander. On one side was the small table with the little green morocco looking-glass—his simple Enlish shaving apparatus—his brushes, combs—a pocket-handkerchief marked Z. 23. On a chair lay a worn military surtout,—beneath were his manly boots. There was something very painful in these relics. If preserved by fraternal affection, it seems strange that the same feeling should not shield them from stranger eyes and touch.

The palace of the Emperor Nicholas, originally built, upon the marriage of her grandson Alexander, by the Empress Catherine, excited very different feelings. It was simpler in decoration than many a noble's at Petersburg, clean as possible, and light with the rays of the bright winter's sun. The only objects on the plain walls of the great drawing-room were a small print of Admiral Sir E. Codrington, and the busts of the seven Imperial children in infantine beauty. The Emperor's own room, in point of heavy writing-tables and bureaux, was that of a man of business, but his military tastes peeped through all. Around on the walls were arranged glass cases containing models of the different cavalry regiments, executed, man and horse, with the greatest beauty, and right, as a military attendant assured us, to a button; and this it seems is the one thing needful. Paintings of military manœuvres and stiff squares of soldiers were also dispersed through his apartments.

Leaving this, we proceeded to the arsenal, a recent red brick erection in English Gothic, in the form of many an old English gatehouse, and a most picturesque object in the most picturesque part of these noble gardens. Here a few weather-beaten veterans reside, who, peeping at our party through the latticed windows, opened the arched doors, and, once within, to an antiquarian eye, all was enchantment. For several successions the Russian sovereigns have amassed a collection of armour and curious antique instruments. These have been increased in the reign of his present Majesty, who erected his building purposely for their reception, and intrusted their classification and arrangement to an Englishman; and truly that gentleman has done credit to the known antiquarian tastes of his own land.

It would be impossible to enumerate the objects here preserved, consisting chiefly of ancient armour, weapons and accoutrements of every description, for man and horse, from every warlike nation both Christian and idolater. Figures in armour guard the entrance and lead the eye along the winding staircase, whence you enter a lofty circular vaulted hall, with oak flooring, and walls hung round with carbines, lances, &c., in fanciful devices, and where, placed on high pedestals in a circle round the room, are eight equestrian figures in full accoutrements and as large as life—like our kings in the Tower. Between these you pass on to various little alcoves or oratories with groined ceiling and stained window, whose light falls on the gorgeously wrought silver cross or precious missal of some early pope—or on the diamond and pearl-woven trappings of present Turkish luxury; or on the hunting-horn, with ivory handle of exquisitely carved figures, of some doughty German Markgraf of the olden time—or on the jousting instruments and other playthings of the amazons of Catherine II.'s court.

But this pleasant arsenal, the only memento in this capital of modern objects and ephemeral fashions which recals the past, would require a volume to itself, and offers inexhaustible interest to the artist in mind, and a very treasury of beautiful subjects to the artist in profession. By command of the Emperor, a most careful and elaborate delineation of its contents, by the best artists of the day, and under the direction of M. Velten of Petersburg, is going forward;—to appear in numbers, of which at present only two have been completed, and of each only two copies printed, the one belonging to his Majesty, the other to Count Benkendorff. These are the most exquisite specimens of drawing and emblazonry, and offer an interest only second to that of the arsenal itself. But the price is high—five hundred roubles a number.

Leaving this building, we passed on through

the extensive gardens of Zarskoe Selo, where a graceful distribution of grounds, though hidden with several feet of snow, and lofty groups of trees, though laden only with the sparkling white foliage of a Russian winter, give presage of the many beauties that summer will awaken. On the one hand was the tower of l' Héritier— an ornamental building in several stories, where this young prince resided with his preceptors, and studied, played, mealed, and slept in different stages. On the other hand were the baby-houses of the young Grand Duchesses, where they carried on a mimic ménage. According to all accounts the childhood of the Imperial children approached nearer to the fairy times of wishing and having than would be well credited. With the bright spirit of perpetual amusement for their mother, and the formidable genius of absolute power for their father, these children seemed to mark the progress of age only by the variety and unlimitedness of their pastimes. This applies, however, more to the daughters of the house, who were the envy of all their juvenile contemporaries: with the sons the application of military discipline formed the boundary of personal indulgence.

It has been the fashion in Russia, and the impression has even crept to foreign countries, to extol the domestic life and habits of the present Imperial family. But it would appear as if the complete familiarity, both between the members of the family itself and in their manners towards others, which the absence of etiquette permits, has been mistaken for a simplicity from which it is far removed. For it is not easy to reconcile the idea of domestic tastes and habits with the entire discouragement of all rational occupations, and the ceaseless thirst for amusement. Of the Empress it is said, as of many other ladies in Petersburg—"*Elle est bonne femme, elle aime ses enfans;*" but now by some in these private circles even this "damning with faint praise" is substituted for less guarded expressions.

As for the Emperor, his high moral character has been the pride of the Russian world; and though much is now whispered to invalidate this opinion, yet, by one of the lightest and prettiest women in the high circles, it was said of him, with an accent of entire sincerity, "*Il ne peut pas être léger; il vous dit tout crument qu'il vous trouve jolie, mais rien de plus.*" Nevertheless, in her Majesty's place, I should rather mistrust this passion for masked balls!

LETTER THE TWENTY-FIFTH.

Visit to the ateliers of Brülloff, Baron Klot, M. Jacques, M. Ladournaire—The Isaac's Church—M. le Maire—Gallery of Prince Belozelsky—Tauride Palace—Church of Smolna, and adjacent institutions — Procession of young girls in court carriages — Winter aspect of the streets—Night drives—Lent, and farewell.

AFTER our expedition to Zarskoe Selo, another day was devoted to seeing those objects in Petersburg which are worthy every traveller's attention, and yet lie not in the traveller's regular routine. We commenced with the ateliers of the different modern artists. In this expedition Prince V. was my escort, whose taste for art is proportioned to the other fine qualities with which Nature has so lavishly gifted him. It was a beautiful day—the thermometer 6° below zero; and yet, wrapped in furs, the still, clear air was not otherwise than agreeable. We first proceeded to the Academy of Arts, on the Wassili-Ostrof, and entered Brülloff's great working-room. Here various studies and half-finished pictures engaged our attention, especially an Ascension of the Virgin, with seraphs and cherubims—a large, arched picture, destined for an altar-piece. However beautiful in form, and orthodox, artistically speaking, in composition, there was something about this picture which indicated rather the restraint than the indulgence of Brülloff's genius, which, to our view, seemed fitted for forms and expressions less celestial, for movements more rapid, and for colouring more florid. And on removing to his lodgings, in another part of the Academy, where, unfortunately, the spirit of the chamber was absent, our surmises were verified; for here, scattered about, were the freer emanations of his pencil: groups of dancing figures, with all the flow of Rubens — sultanas couched in every languid attitude—animals, elephants and dogs—all touched with that freedom and fire which forms the chief charm of his great picture, the

Fall of Pompeii. Brülloff's personal character is not good. According to my noble companion's brief sentence—"*Brülloff est comme Guido, méchant homme, mais grand artiste.*"

Thence to the atelier of Baron Klot, an Estonian nobleman and old militaire, who, as if his genius had slumbered till the evening of life should give it leisure, has, without the advantages of foreign study, produced works in sculpture surpassed by no modern artist. A bronze horse, in full action, with lion's skin and paws hanging over, restrained by a standing figure, in equal energy and development of form, was fit to take its place by the side of Falconnet's statue of Peter the Great, and offered in every aspect the grandest outline. On the floor, in the act of gilding, lay figures of seraphs, with expanded wings, ten feet in height, destined to surround the upper dome of St. Isaac's Church, whither a few of these statues have already taken flight, looking from below scarce larger than golden eagles.

From Baron Klot's most interesting studio we passed on to that of M. Jacques, another sculptor, now engaged on a colossal figure of Peter the Great, thirty feet high, placed on a pedestal, with a truncheon in his hand, which, when cast in bronze, is to occupy a conspicuous position at the entrance of Cronstadt harbour. We surprised M. Jacques at his work, who showed us the utmost courtesy and attention.

The room of M. Ladournaire, a painter of portraits and subject-pictures, next claimed our attention. The principal object of attraction was a large picture, painted by command of the Emperor, representing the inauguration of the Alexander's column, on which occasion a review of a hundred thousand troops took place. On the right is the Winter Palace, treated, as the character of its architecture warrants, in the Canaletti manner. For that day, a temporary balcony from the second floor of the palace, with awnings, and a magnificent sweep of steps on either hand, was erected; where are seen the persons of the Empress and her court, and where, though reduced to figures not above an inch long, we recognised many acquaintances. On the left is seen the column in question, and between these two chief objects is the dusty review —the figures of the Emperor, with Count Benkendorff and others of his general aides-de-camp, in the foreground. Considering the disadvantage of the subject, M. Ladournaire has rendered it unusually picturesque and interesting.

Another subject of greater interest was that of the Héritier taking the oaths of allegiance to his father on attaining his twenty-first year. On this occasion the young prince showed much of that gentleness of nature which his countenance evinces; and when he came to the words "*et quand le Seigneur m'enlevera mon père,*" his emotion almost overcame him. All unite in extolling the kindness of heart and gentleness of spirit with which the Héritier of Russia is endowed.

This Academy seems in every way to carry out the intention of its foundress. The various ateliers we had visited, all spacious and appropriate, are furnished by this institution to its members, while the education and foreign study of every pupil of promise is also given gratuitously.

We now retraced our steps over the Isaac's bridge, and entered the circle of temporary buildings with which the great Isaac's Church, which the Russians already designate as the *Sabor*, or cathedral, is surrounded. Never was pure Corinthian seen beneath so piercing a climate; and yet the clearness and transparency of the atmosphere were such, that, to the organ of vision alone, it might have been mistaken for the heated and glowing sky of Greece. This building is in the form of an equal cross, with four grand entrances, approached by a flight of granite steps, each whole flight in one entire piece; but, after the Alexander's column, this is nothing for Petersburg. We entered the transept fronting the Neva, which is also the most advanced towards completion. This alone is a building of enormous magnitude, on too large a scale for us human pigmies, unless we except this magnificent Emperor. The vastness of the whole edifice, when completed, may therefore be conjectured. The original design of the cathedral at Cologne is not nearly so gigantic. The embellishments of the façade and windows are intrusted to other sculptors, who share with those we have mentioned in this grand task. The atelier of M. le Maire, a French sculptor engaged for this purpose, was close by; the department assigned to him is the group of figures on the pediment of one of the façades—the subject the Angel at the Tomb, with the Magdalen and other female figures on the one side, and the terrified soldiers, in every attitude of consternation, on the other: the figures eight feet in height. These are all to be in bronze, gilt over, though, to increase the relief of the figures, M. le Maire intends suggesting to the Imperial sanction whether it would not be expedient to leave the back-ground of the pediment the colour of the metal.

Having thus taken an aggregate of the artists whom Russia has sent forth from her own academy, or summoned from others, we bent our course along the length of the Nevsky to the residence of Prince Belozélsky. This nobleman possesses a fine gallery of paintings, collected by his father, a connoisseur of established fame, during a long residence in Italy. A splendid Guido, Mercury and Flora strewing the distant earth with roses, and drawn with cords by fluttering Cupids, is the chef-d'œuvre of the collection. A small sketch by Raphael of the Murder of the Innocents appeared to me to possess all the beauties of that master. Two Gaspar Poussins, two Breughels of unusual size, were among the most remarkable. But the gallery is in great disorder, and, being unheated, the pictures are suffering from the inclemency of the atmosphere. Princess Belozelsky, whose beauty I have before alluded to, is now sitting to Mrs. Robinson, our English artist, who is earning golden opinions in the high circles for the beauty and grace of her portraits. This lady is also engaged upon a full-length of the Empress.

Hence we proceeded to the Tauride Palace, presented by Potemkin to Catherine II.—the latest sovereign on European record who has accepted such a gift from a favourite. This building is now dedicated to the residence of a few superannuated ladies of the court. The entrance saloon is occupied by a collection of antique marbles; and in the centre stands a temple, in form like the temple of Vesta, with malachite pillars and inlaid jasper floor, capable of containing about six persons, and destined, not as the seat (for in Russian houses of worship none sit), but as the standing-place of honour of the Emperor—to be included within that most worthy outer temple the Isaac's Church: this is the gift of M. Demidoff. Through the Salle des Antiques we passed to the grand ball-room,—where Potemkin gave a fête to the Empress, and where the musicians were suspended in the chandeliers,—which terminates in a vast semicircle, filled with orange and pomegranate trees, interspersed with marble statues.

The church of Smolna now claimed our attention—a magnificent pile in white marble, with *les institutions pour les filles nobles* on either hand, each with chapel adjoining, on the same scale as the church, and connected with a gorgeous iron railing. We entered,—and the peculiarity of the scene arrested our steps—for no object met our view save walls and columns of polished, dazzling white marble. Passing on, the three altars appeared, or rather the massive screens, of bronze-gilt vine-leaves, grapes, and ears of corn intertwined, which concealed them. The altar-steps and pavement were of porphyry, the altar-railings crystal.

A velvet canopy on the one hand betokens the Emperor's place, and on the other a marble tablet records the benevolent life of the late Empress-mother, who founded the adjoining institutions. But these were the only objects which broke the grand monotony of white marble. The choristers sing from the heights of the pillars, the narrow overhanging ledge being protected by invisible railings. The church was of a most agreeable temperature (or rather where is the Russian edifice that is not?)—this is maintained by twenty-four stoves, heated without intermission.

Emerging, we encountered thirty of the

court carriages, in grand trappings, proceeding at a foot-pace, and bearing the young ladies of the adjoining convents, who on this only day of the year parade slowly through the streets, and are allowed to have such a peep of the world as may be had through the clouded glasses of a coach, and in the presence of a superior. Four of these young creatures were in each coach, attended by an elder.

And now by this time we were almost as sick of sight-seeing as, doubtless, you are; and with sharpened appetites, cloaks laden with icicles, and cheeks tinged with the brightest crimson, we returned to the luxurious mansions of the great in Petersburg.

However we may impugn the severity and implacability of a Russian frost, yet there is something inexpressibly exhilarating in this continuance of serene, sunny weather, which sheds a hazy brightness over the picturesque street and canal scenery of this capital, and decks the distant snow perspective in alternate stripes of yellow lights and lilac shadows. As many sledges are now seen gliding upon the canals as in the streets—as many passing under as crossing over the numerous bridges. A constant warfare, however, is going forward with the ice; for bands of peasants are hewing and extracting great blocks—destined for the summer's ice-houses, or intended to alleviate the violence of the thaw's inundation,—and thence are seen filing through the streets on rough sledges, composedly leaning or sitting on their cold, transparent loads.

There is a peculiar pleasure in passing from one quarter of this vast capital to another by night, in an open sledge, with one fiery horse and a trusty coachman, crossing from the islands, the gloomy Neva, which is lighted by lamps, just directing your track; with the huge outline, spiked with scaffolding, of the Isaac's Church rising dull against the sky, and the Winter Palace before you streaked with brightly lighted arched windows, framed in yellow or crimson draperies. Thence through the streets, less lighted by their oil-lamps than by the illuminated palaces of the nobility; while here and there a crush of carriages, and bright flaring tongues of flames from vessels of oil placed on the pavement, betoken a gala within. And so onwards through the Champ de Mars; on the one hand, the flickering, shooting coruscations of an aurora, bright as the rising sun, the almost nightly phenomenon of this latitude—and on the other the glare of a fire in the suburbs, which, from the number of old wooden houses still left, and the proverbial Russian carelessness, is almost as frequent an occurrence. And now the horse rushes swiftly forward, disturbing thoughts which have wandered, they know not how, from these fires of heaven and earth to homes in England, and that scarce less than home in Estonia; and the air meets your face with the sharpness of an instrument, while, regardless of the deep furrows of the long-worn ice, the generous animal continues his speed till the little sledge mounts and descends like a bark on a bounding wave; and you are fain to hook one finger into the coachman's broad silken belt to keep your equilibrium.

At all fires of any importance, the Emperor,

who appears to perform the real labour of any three men in his own person, and to possess a frame and a will of the same metal, is a constant attendant. Also here, as at the masked balls, some of his principal officers are summoned as a part of their service; sometimes with such trial, from fatigue and exposure to cold, to their physical powers, as to induce the unloyal wish that his Majesty's were a little less vigorous.

But it seems a prevailing principle with the Crown to interpose its presence, or an earnest of its presence, in every circumstance of life, whether usual or accidental,—to prove to its subjects the indispensability of its help—to maintain literally the relation of parent and child—and by retaining its hold over every department, and making that a favour which we should consider a right, to facilitate the immediate exertion of its power. With the army this is conspicuously the case. The officer whose strict pay is so paltry that it is far from defraying the expenses of his wife's wardrobe, receives in addition what is called

Tafel-geld, or table-money: for, like the soldiers, he is supposed to be boarded at the Emperor's expense, and besides this may expect an annual present, either from his Majesty or the Grand Duke Michael, equal about in amount to his pay. Lodging and furniture are also provided him. The higher officers connected with the state, especially, occupy magnificent residences belonging to the Crown, and furnished with proportionate splendour. Such is the extent of Count ———'s superb hotel, one of the Crown residences just mentioned, that a subaltern constantly resides in the house in order to superintend the necessary repairs. If a chimney smokes, or a window is broken, or a nail requires to be placed, this crown servant is summoned.

But these subjects, trivial as they may appear, are connected with the very well-springs of Russian policy, and therefore not within the vocation of these letters. Meanwhile, the Carnival, or what is here termed the *Maslenitza*—literally the *Butterwoche*, or Butter-week—when the fatiguing round of amusement is redoubled

—when masked balls are more frequent and more full—when the theatres are open both morning and evening—when the grand *Place* before the Winter Palace is occupied by the *Montagnes Russes*, and by the *Katcheli*, or Russian merry-go-rounds—and when the streets throng with that unusual feature in Petersburg, a crowd of pedestrians—this happy time for so many is come and gone; and in its place, Lent, with its church-going and fasting—when concerts and tableaux constitute the sole entertainments—when the German theatre alone is open —when meat and butter, eggs and milk, are all forbidden, and your tea and coffee are only mollified by the extract of almonds—when all the outward apparel of a feast goes forward, but your dishes are only an ingenious variation of fish and oil, flour and water; or if a more nutritious ingredient, or more savoury taste, find its way in, it is at the expense of the cook's conscience, and not your own;—Lent, when those who before had feasted, or before had starved, all now equally fast, and from which only the foreigner or the invalid is exempt, has now commenced its seven weeks' reign.

And with the vanished gaieties of this gayest and dullest of all capitals the sober writer of these letters must also pass away—to retain a sincere admiration for the intrinsic elements of Russia—the deepest interest in its welfare—the highest faith in its destiny;—but also the reluctant conviction that, at this present time, Russia is the country where the learned man wastes his time, the patriot breaks his heart, and the rogue prospers.

THE END.

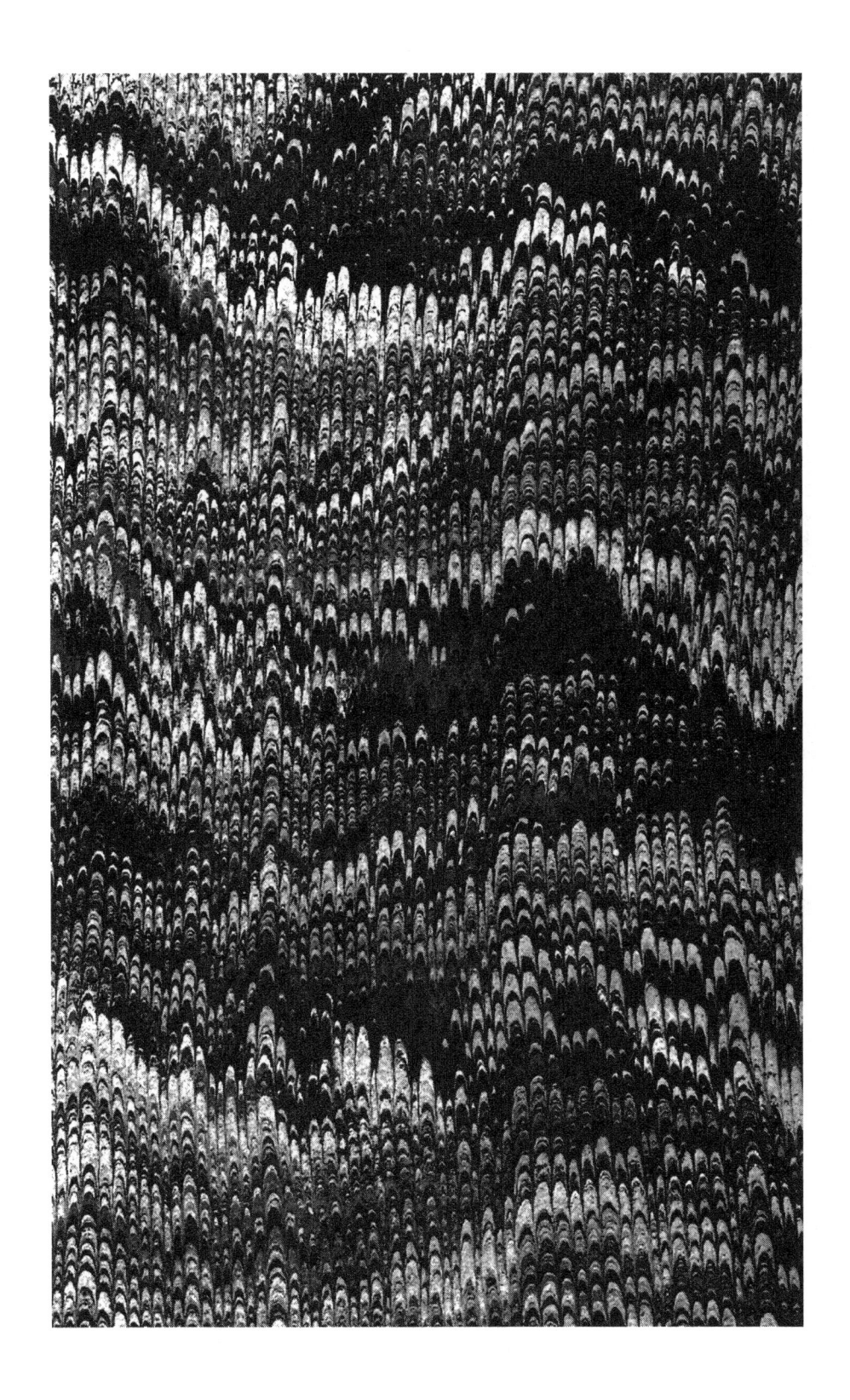

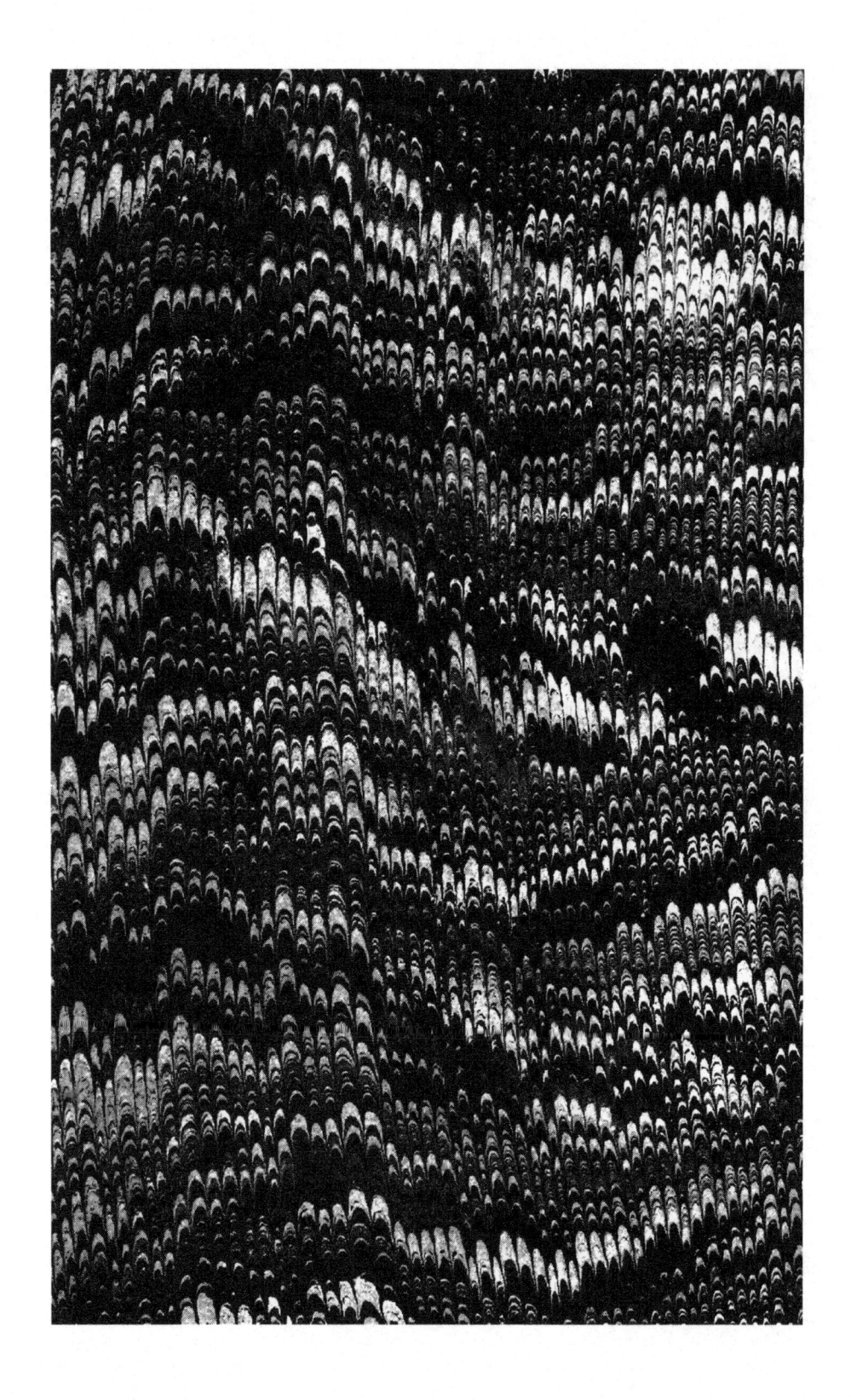